'This book could not be more timely. I believe [it is one of the most] important parenting books of our time. If you are a parent, carer, [or work] with children in any capacity, I would urge you to read it.'

Rob Parsons OBE, Founder and Chairman, Care for the Family.

'In the 15 years I have been working with and parenting traumatised children in care, I have seen first hand how vital it is to provide mental health support and to nurture resilience – even for the very youngest of our children. In a post-Covid world, where all children everywhere have experienced trauma, disruption and insecurity to some extent, Katharine Hill's book is more important than ever. It offers so many hopeful and practical ideas and I commend it warmly.'

Dr Krish Kandiah, Author, social entrepreneur and Chair of the Adoption and Special Guardianship Leadership Board.

'Authoritative and actionable, with every chapter subtly steeped in the science of mental wellbeing and distress, Katharine Hill breathes confidence into parents that they have what it takes to help their children grow into emotionally healthy adults.'

Dr Samantha Callan, Director, Family Hubs Network.

'As a psychologist and a Mum, I can confirm the latter is much harder! Reading this is like sitting down with a wonderfully experienced, well informed, beautifully calm and practical friend. Full of practical tips as well as empathy and stories shared by many other parents who have journeyed through things before you, it will help you hold your nerve when times are hard, and give you great ideas for positive steps to open up possibilities and break unhelpful patterns so you can feel more in control and help your children model healthy emotions and learn the skills they need to navigate the complex but exciting world they are growing up in.'

Dr Kate Middleton, Psychologist and Director of the Mind and Soul Foundation.

'We have known Katharine for many years and have seen that she has practised what she writes about. Any parent will find her advice easy to read and her practical suggestions difficult to ignore. A Mind of their Own is both important and timely. It is full of ideas that any parent can implement to bring small changes to their family life that can have a huge impact on their child's wellbeing. We recommend it to every parent who wants to help their child develop character, emotional resilience and healthy relationships.'

Nicky and Sila Lee, co-authors of The Parenting Book
and The Marriage Book.

'It has never been more important to think about children's resilience and well-being and this book is a great place to start. Katharine Hill has delved into the psychological literature so that you don't have to. The result is a short and punchy overview of the evidence that stays firmly rooted in the realities of family life. All served up with wisdom, common sense and lots of practical suggestions. What more could you ask for?'

Glynn Harrison, Emeritus Professor of Psychiatry, University of Bristol and retired consultant psychiatrist.

A MIND OF
THEIR OWN

A MIND OF
THEIR OWN

KATHARINE HILL

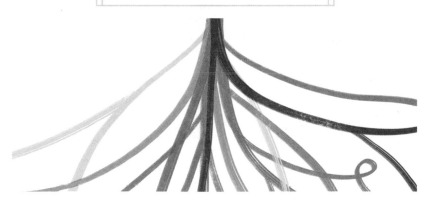

Muddy
Pearl

Published in 2021 by
Muddy Pearl, Edinburgh, Scotland.
www.muddypearl.com
books@muddypearl.com

British Library Cataloguing in Publication Data
A catalogue record for this book is available from the British Library

ISBN 978-1-910012-31-4

Typeset in Minion by Revo Creative Ltd, Lancaster
Printed in Great Britain by Bell & Bain Ltd, Glasgow

For my sister Elisabeth –
one of the most resilient people I know.

FOREWORD

Young people are the future. So how important must it be to make sure they grow up mentally healthy and flourishing? This means both the absence of specific traumas and unnecessary stress, but also the presence of good mental health and an excitement about what lies ahead.

However, what it means to grow up seems to have changed overnight. Much of life now is happening online, especially since the outbreak of COVID-19, and instant accessibility to almost all information humans own poses additional risks. How can we parent in a way that nurtures our children's emotional wellbeing with all this going on?

In this groundbreaking book, Katharine Hill, the UK Director of Care for the Family, brings a fresh and helpful look at how we can best equip our children in this area. In my work, I often see people once they have been mentally ill for some time, and I wonder if things would have been different if they had got help sooner. This book isn't about defining mental illness or how to treat clinical conditions, but it is about key strategies for parents that we know work in the home, at school and in everyday life.

It is also about putting this topic on the table. We can't talk about flourishing families without talking about good mental health. And, once the issue isn't made taboo or treated dismissively, it is much easier for the child or young person to speak up about any struggles they may be having. We cannot have situations where they wonder if their emotions are 'OK' or if the possibility of failure will be allowed.

And finally, it's about being honest with each other, to admit that we are in a new era of parenting, and to commit to journeying with others. The material that Katharine has so helpfully provided in this book is a great place to start.

DR ROB WALLER MA MSc MBBCh FRCPsych

Edinburgh, January 2021

Dr Rob Waller is a Consultant Psychiatrist working for the NHS in Scotland and a Director of The Mind and Soul Foundation.

PREFACE

In my work as UK Director of the charity Care for the Family, I have become increasingly aware of the growing pressure on family life today. While media reports of rising referrals and overstretched mental health services are troubling, what has moved my heart to breaking is hearing real-life stories of parents who feel helpless as they watch their happy, easy-going children being overwhelmed by a tsunami of pressure and anxiety. Real concerns about the wellbeing of stressed 6-year-olds and frazzled 15-year-olds are keeping parents up at night.

I began to write this book as a response to that need, wanting to put messages of confidence and hope in parents' hands for the season ahead. That was at the end of 2019.

Enter 2020.

Could anyone have foreseen how quickly the world was about to change? At the beginning of the year, perhaps most of us would not have heard of Wuhan, the city in Central China where the pandemic is believed to have originated. But within weeks it seemed to be mentioned in every news bulletin as the COVID-19 virus spread across the world and our lives were turned upside down. 'Social distancing', 'shielding', and 'self-isolation' became household words. Shopping malls emptied, schools and businesses closed, and family life at home 24/7 became the new normal. With the death toll continuing to rise, many are suffering the trauma of losing family members to the disease. And although everyone has been affected, the pandemic has dealt a very heavy blow to our children's emotional wellbeing, and, in some cases, their already fragile mental health.

As I read through my draft manuscript, I realized two things. The first was that the pandemic has thrown up a whole new set of challenges and pressures for families to navigate, and so I decided to write a special chapter simply focused on unpacking the impact of COVID-19 on our children's wellbeing. Second, I realized that the principles in this book are timeless. Taken and applied in the context of the pandemic and its aftermath, they will help develop resilience and emotional wellbeing in our children at a time when they need it most.

A 'liminal space' is a phrase used to describe a waiting area between one point in time and space and the next – the threshold between the old season and the new. COVID-19 has catapulted all of us into such a space, unsettling family routines, and forcing us to realign our priorities and recalibrate our lives. For many, it is a difficult space, but it has given us the rare opportunity to take stock of our lives – to pause and think about what things are important to us. In particular, we have the opportunity to consider how, in post-pandemic life, we can prioritize the things that will build our children's emotional resilience and enable them to step into the future with confidence and hope.

KATHARINE HILL

Bristol, January 2021

ACKNOWLEDGEMENTS

This has been a challenging book to write and simply would not have been possible without the wisdom and input of so many people.

First, thank you to Rob Parsons and to Care for the Family's Senior Editor, Sheron Rice. The proverb says 'Iron sharpens iron'; thank you for the vital role you played in the honing process, and Sheron for your superb editing skills.

Thank you to Samantha Callan and to Nick Philps for expertly compiling the research that underpins this book, and Nick also for your careful editing and continual encouragement.

I am grateful to those who read and commented on the manuscript, particularly Rob Waller and Kate Middleton, and to Rob for writing the foreword.

A huge thank you to the wonderful teams at Care for the Family and at Muddy Pearl, and especially to Stephanie Heald.

Thanks also to David McNeill who once again lifts the copy with his great cartoons.

I am especially grateful to those families who so generously shared their experiences of joy and struggle in the ups and downs of family life. I have changed details so you remain anonymous, but your stories make all the difference and ground this book in reality.

And last but by no means least thank you to my own family – Richard, George, Ellie and Eva, Charlotte, Will and Ezra, Ed and Catriona, and Henry. The family is the best place to learn so many of life's lessons, and I love still learning so much from you all!

CONTENTS

'I don't understand how it was so much better when you were younger AND you think I have it easy?'

CHAPTER 1

YOU WERE NEVER THEIR AGE

It was one of those moments that nobody in the room will forget. A child psychologist was talking to a group of parents about what she was seeing in the young people who came to her for counselling and the special pressures she felt they were under. A woman who had already been pretty vocal in a question-and-answer session suddenly interrupted: 'I think some of them just need to toughen up at bit,' she declared. 'When I was their age ...'

She never did get to finish the sentence because the psychologist put up her hand – a clear signal to her to stop – and said very slowly and deliberately:

'Madam, you were *never* their age.'

I think the psychologist was right. Behind her words lay the realization that our children are growing up in a fast-changing world, light years away from the one most of us grew up in. Some of the unique pressures they are facing were graphically illustrated in a campaign by The Children's Society in which an online 'shop' displayed objects designed to reflect modern childhood.[1] The iconic items exhibited included a child's stab vest, a self-hate notebook containing dark thoughts, anxiety concealer make-up, and mobile phone cases covered in messages of fear and worry to represent the threat of cyberbullying. That was before the pandemic presented them with the challenge of schools being closed for months, having to deal with online and blended learning and the uncertainty of cancelled exams.

In my work at Care for the Family, every week I hear from parents who are dealing with the challenges – both small and great – of bringing up children in today's world.

- 5-year-old Ben has started school. He's worried about the end of term tests and has started wetting the bed again.

- 9-year-old Rosie sees her dad every weekend but has become clingy and developed a nervous tic since he moved out.

- 11-year-old Andre has been feeling the pressure ever since his mum told him that as a black boy he will need to work harder and play harder than his white friends if he is to succeed in life.

- 12-year-old Kareena is having nightmares about the future of the planet. She campaigns about climate change on social media, joins marches and strikes to demand urgent action, but feels overwhelmed by the scale of the problem.

- 13-year-old Hailey was given a smartphone for her birthday. She knows she doesn't look her best in the photo she's just taken, but she posts it on her social media account anyway. Later, she sees that one of her friends has drawn red rings around her freckles.

---

1 Monica Greep, 'Shocking images of children wearing STAB vests over school uniforms sweep social media as part of a hard-hitting charity campaign', *Daily Mail Online*, 31 August 2019, dailymail.co.uk.

- 14-year-old Mia is confused about her identity and wonders if she may be trans. She is worried about talking to her parents about this. Her friend has started self-harming and said that it helps her feel in control. Yesterday, on the way home from school, Mia bought some razor blades.

- 15-year-old Liane gets together with her friends after the exam and talks about how badly she's done. A few weeks later, she is inconsolable when she misses an A grade by two points.

- 16-year-old Jack is smaller than his peers. He has joined a gym and works out fanatically, obsessing over pictures of bodybuilders on Instagram and spending all of his money on body-building protein shakes.

- 17-year-old Bella is worried about the future and whether she will be able to get a job. She has been told she can do anything, but she feels the pressure to be everything.

While this list is enough to make any parent feel concerned, it's not all bad news. We certainly don't have to stand by helplessly wringing our hands and looking wistfully back to a bygone era. Our children are growing up in world of incredible opportunity. The digital age means that at the touch of a screen they have access to a world of information and the possibility of connections and relationships across the world. There are increasing opportunities to study, and many young people are far more socially and globally aware than previous generations at a similar age.

The challenge our children face is how to navigate this complex world full of both opportunity and challenge, potential and risk. In this, we can take heart from the fact that the people most able to help them are us, their parents. But if we are to do this, it's not enough for us to be aware of the potential issues and their impact on mental health. We also need to know what action we can take to help our children be confident, resilient and emotionally healthy adults.

Before considering what, as parents, we can do, let's first take a brief look at the issues and the extent of the problem. Young people's mental health has attracted increasing media focus in the last few years, even before the pandemic. Hardly a week would go by without attention-grabbing news headlines about escalating numbers of children with mental illness:

Young people's mental health is a 'worsening crisis'.[2]

Surge in children seeking mental health support from cash-strapped councils ...[3]

Mental health problems among children have hit 'crisis point', say teachers.[4]

Child mental health unit referrals up nearly 50%.[5]

Ten thousand young people on mental health waiting lists.[6]

Research commissioned by the NHS found that one in eight 5- to 19-year-olds now have at least one mental health disorder. That's at least three in every classroom.[7] Nine out of ten children, some as young as 11, worry about 'adult issues' including climate change, poverty, homelessness, terrorism and inequality; while four in

2 Mary O'Hara, 'Young people's mental health is a "worsening crisis". Action is needed', *The Guardian*, 31 July 2018, guardian.com.
3 Mary Bulman, 'Surge in children seeking mental health support from cash-strapped councils, figures show', *The Independent*, 30 June 2019, independent.co.uk.
4 Amy Packham, 'Mental Health Problems Among Children Have Hit "Crisis Point", Say Teachers', *Huffington Post*, 17 April 2019, huffingtonpost.co.uk.
5 Noel Titheradge and Ed Thomas, 'Child mental health unit referrals up nearly 50%', *BBC News*, 18 July 2019, bbc.co.uk.
6 Katrine Bussey, 'Ten thousand young people on mental health waiting lists', *The Times*, 4 December 2019, thetimes.co.uk.
7 'Mental Health of Children and Young People in England, 2017', *NHS Digital*, November 2018, digital.nhs.co.uk.

ten add Brexit, sexism and racism to their list.[8] And if that wasn't enough, the impact of the COVID-19 world pandemic has added another layer of deep concern. Although, as yet, the ongoing effects are unknown, they are likely to to be part of our children's future.

Moving the lens away from global issues, many of the burdens on young people are much closer to home. The particular pressures that many black and other ethnic minority children and young people face have come into even greater focus after recent tragic events. A third of 10- to 17-year-olds worry about having enough money in the future, and more than a quarter worry about getting a job.[9] School life focuses on targets and rankings, and life in general has become increasingly competitive – even the fun stuff. It's no longer enough simply to do their best and enjoy life; young people feel under pressure to *be* the best. Add to this the well-documented worries about family breakdown, body image and relationships, and (ironically) mental health – all exacerbated by the pressures of technology and social media – and we have a perfect storm.

The issues are complex, yet it's interesting to note that the rise in anxiety and depression among young people has coincided with the introduction of the smartphone.[10] The digital age has certainly brought us many advantages: at any time of the day or night we can order a pizza, check our bank balance, watch a film, or connect with family and friends. For our young people, the online world is where social dramas are played out, where relationships are built, and a place where they can access support, follow their interests, and discover more about the world.

8 Nigel Barlow, 'Childhood in crisis: Almost two thirds of parents and grandparents say childhood getting worse – and nearly two million children in the UK agree', *Action for Children*, 9 July 2019, actionforchildren.org.uk.
9 'The Good Childhood Report 2020', *The Children's Society*, September 2020, childrenssociety.org.uk.
10 Jean M. Twenge, *iGen: Why Today's Super-Connected Kids Are Growing Up Less Rebellious, More Tolerant, Less Happy – and Completely Unprepared for Adulthood* (Atria Books, 2017), p111.

But the many advantages of our always-on culture come at a price. Family life is now permeable with 24/7 connectivity bringing real-time news bulletins. And whether it's a suicide bomber at a pop concert, a terrorist attack on London Bridge, images of people fleeing their flooded homes, or footage from hospital wards showing COVID-19 patients struggling to breathe, our children hear and see all the details.

New research has found, perhaps unsurprisingly, that the more time young teenagers spend on social media the greater the impact on their mental wellbeing. The Millennium Cohort Study found that the average 13- to 15-year-old spends one to three hours on social media every day.[11] Our brains are highly tuned to social acceptance and rejection, and the need to accumulate likes and followers means that for the first time in history our children have a number allocated to their worth. Social media provides fertile soil for anxiety and other negative emotions, particularly among those who are the most vulnerable to mental health issues. It is ironic that reducing use of social media has been found to make young people feel less lonely.[12]

While many of us will remember that heart-sinking feeling of arriving at school on a Monday morning and realizing we hadn't been included in the weekend trip to town or to the beach, today's child can watch the event unfold in real time, selfie by selfie.

Cyberbullying is prolific. In a YouGov survey of 5,000 children, parents and grandparents, bullying was cited as the biggest impediment to a good childhood as children deal with it both on- and offline.[13] And Instagram highlights that magnify issues surrounding appearance and body image, combined with a lack of

11 Holly Scott et al, 'Social media use and adolescent sleep patterns: cross-sectional findings from the Millennium Cohort Study', *BMJ Open*, vol.9, no.9, 2019, bmjopen.com.
12 Jean M. Twenge, *iGen*, p83.
13 Nigel Barlow, 'Childhood in crisis'.

strong friendships, are driving factors for plummeting happiness levels – for boys now as well as girls.[14]

This toxic trend of unhappiness was highlighted in 'The Good Childhood Report'[15] which discovered a significant decrease in average happiness for 10- to 15-year-olds in the UK. It found that our 15-year-olds are among the saddest and least satisfied with their lives in Europe. Julie Bentley, chief executive of the national charity Action for Children, said: 'The country is sleepwalking into a crisis in childhood, and far from being carefree, our children are buckling under the weight of unprecedented social pressures, [and] global turmoil.'[16]

While we are clearly living in unprecedented times, opinion has been divided on whether there is indeed a mental health epidemic or whether we are, in fact, overreacting and the younger generation simply need to toughen up and stop being snowflakes. Student mental health specialist Dr Dominique Thompson argues that both of these views are unhelpful: 'There is no epidemic, and the young are not (on the whole) overreacting, but they have been raised in a very different society, and this has led to very different outcomes for them.'[17]

We use the term *emotional wellbeing* to refer to the quality of our emotional experience – the barometer of how we think, feel and relate to others and also to ourselves. Our emotional wellbeing affects how we see and understand the world, and it is an important part of our overall health. People who are emotionally healthy are able to cope with life's challenges, keep problems in perspective and bounce back from setbacks. Poor emotional wellbeing, on the other hand, is related to mental health concerns such as anxiety and depression, which can also affect our overall physical health and

14 Gabriella Swerling, 'Social media and body image are making our children the unhappiest for 25 years', *The Telegraph,* 28 August 2019, telegraph.co.uk.
15 'The Good Childhood Report,' 2020.
16 Nigel Barlow, 'Childhood in crisis'.
17 Dominique Thompson and Fabienne Vailes, *How to Grow a Grown Up: Prepare your teen for the real world,* (Ebury Digital, 2019), p246.

set back the emotional growth of young children, stopping them from making friends, taking part in social activities, sitting exams successfully and fulfilling their potential.

When our children are little, we encourage their physical growth and take precautions to keep them safe. We limit sugar and encourage healthy eating, establish appropriate bedtimes, regulate screen time, install stair gates, child locks and car seats, and teach them to swim and to cross the road safely. And it's important to be equally intentional about helping them grow emotionally strong and healthy. Just as they get a few bumps and bruises on the outside, they will inevitably get a few knocks inside as well.

Of course, there are no guarantees. Mental ill health can occur for all kinds of reasons, and if we suspect that our children are suffering from serious anxiety or depression, or that they are at risk of self-harm, it's important to seek the advice of a GP or other professional.

Before we begin, let me make two general observations. First, research underpins this book and I have used scientific evidence in relation to the brain to illustrate particular points. However, it's important to acknowledge that scientists have been trying to understand how the brain works for centuries; it's an extraordinary organ and we are still far from fully understanding its complexity.

Second, I have written this book to help all parents and children, but I am very aware of the extra and complex challenges of families where there are children with additional needs and where parents are dealing with other very difficult parenting issues. At Care for the Family, in our projects to encourage and support parents of children with additional needs, I am continually humbled and inspired by their courage, strength and resilience. My hope and prayer is that you are able to take and apply the principles of the book in a way that meets the needs of your individual family.

Along with key principles for parents with regard to nurturing their child's resilience, this book gives parents messages that we can pass on to our children. Weaving these messages into our children's consciousness can buffer them against life's challenges and build a solid foundation of emotional wellbeing.

Our goal isn't to bring up children; it is to bring up adults who are confident, resilient and secure in their identity – adults who have *a mind of their own*. And we – their parents – are well placed to do this. Libraries of research demonstrate that we really are the biggest influence on their lives.

We have everything to play for!

'These rules aren't fair. I've been monitoring your screen time,
and you're on for over seven hours a day!'

CHAPTER 2

FAMILY MATTERS

There are all kinds of families in all kinds of situations. There are couples who are parenting together and those who are parenting apart. There are families with single parents, adoptive parents, foster parents, step-parents and grandparents. But whatever its shape or size, and whether just at the moment our children are a delight or whether they are breaking our hearts, the one thing that unites every family is that it provides the best place for the foundations for life to be laid. The most important learning takes place in the home. It's the place where we learn to relate to one another, appreciate our differences, manage conflict, and handle power; the place where we learn to forgive and be forgiven, to love and to be loved. Indeed, according to Winston Churchill: 'There is no doubt that it is around the family and the home that all the greatest virtues, the most dominating virtues of human society, are created, strengthened and maintained'.[18]

Family dynamics matter to a child's emotional wellbeing. Research has found that growing up in a nurturing, supportive and stable

18 Winston Churchill, 'House of Commons Debate: Birth of A Prince (Address of Congratulation)', *Hansard*, vol.458, col. 211, 16 November 1948, hansard.parliament.uk.

environment is a key factor in helping young people to manage stress,[19] develop resilience,[20] build trust, and navigate life's challenges.

I often remind mums and dads who attend our Care for the Family parenting events that over and above their role as nappy-changer, packed-lunch-maker, sports-kit-washer, homeworker-helper, taxi-provider and a million other jobs besides, their most important role is to be the 'keeper of the atmosphere' in the home. We know that we have an active part to play in giving our children a healthy, safe home environment, but this role is not simply to read the thermometer – it is to *set* the thermostat of the emotional temperature in our home. The atmosphere we create as parents will have a significant impact on our children's wellbeing. As the old proverb says, 'You reap what you sow', and a negative atmosphere will have a negative effect. A home that is unstable and chaotic, and where there is disruption, intolerance and volatility, is a source of stress and a heavy emotional weight for children to carry. On the other hand, children growing up in a positive environment of interest, respect, clear boundaries and love are more likely to develop healthy self-esteem and confidence in themselves.[21, 22]

Creating a positive atmosphere doesn't happen in a vacuum; it takes place in the context of the whole family dynamic, including in the midst of the cares and troubles of life. Research shows that parents who can create a sense of optimism in spite of major

19 Young Ran Tak and Marilyn McCubbin, 'Family stress, perceived social support and coping following the diagnosis of a child's congenital heart disease', *National Library of Medicine*, (39)2, 27 July 2002, pubmed.ncbi.nlm.nih.gov.
20 Deborah O'Donnell, Mary Schwab-Stone and Adaline Muyeed, 'Multidimensional Resilience in Urban Children Exposed to Community Violence', *Child Development*, 73(4), July – August 2002, pp1265–1282.
21 Samantha Krauss, Ulrich Orth and Richard Robins, 'Family Environment and Self-Esteem Development: A Longitudinal Study from Age 10 to 16', *Journal of Personality and Social Psychology*, 119(2), January 2020, pp457–478.
22 'Family Atmosphere: How Does it Influence Children's Upbringing', *Exploring Your Mind*, 18 August 2019, exploringyourmind.com.

difficulties or setbacks are more likely to create an environment in the home where children can flourish.[23]

We live in a house that was once in the countryside but is now in the heart of Bristol due to suburban sprawl. A few years ago, there was an unexpected knock at the door and two smiling older gentlemen greeted us. They told us they had lived in our house when they were growing up and delighted our children with tales of going down the lane (now the path to a school) to milk the cows and making butter in the kitchen by turning the handle on the milk churn. As they left, one of them made a remark that has stayed with me ever since. He said, 'This was always a happy house. Noisy, but full of children laughing'.

Looking back, I can think of many occasions when the atmosphere in our house was noisy – but in a 'nuclear' rather than 'nurturing' way. We all mess up, and no doubt all of us can think of times when we've lost the plot under stress. We've been too hard or too soft with our children; too controlling or too laid back. Sometimes we have simply not been present – physically or emotionally – when they needed us. But this is about the bigger picture, and if any of our offspring return to visit their childhood home in fifty years' time, while they may remember moments of stress and sadness, I would be sad if they didn't remember the noise of the fun and laughter.

Psychologist John Bowlby's research in the 1950s and 1960s into attachment has become key to understanding child development. Attachment is a deep and enduring bond that connects one person to another, and Bowlby showed that the development of this bond, even from the womb, is vital to a child's emotional security. The most important principle of attachment theory is that for normal social and emotional development, young children need to develop

---

23 'Wellbeing Factsheets: 04', *Institute of Wellbeing*, 2017, foundationyears.org.uk.

a relationship with at least one primary caregiver.[24] This relationship – or lack of it – significantly impacts their whole lives. As parents or carers, when we respond to a baby's need to be fed, comforted, kept warm or stimulated, the baby learns that they are both loved and loveable.[25]

The amazing thing is that the quality of this nurturing relationship actually affects the physical development of the brain. Sobering pictures demonstrate the shockingly smaller and less developed regions of the brains of children who have suffered severe neglect compared to children who have been nurtured and loved.[26] The implications are significant: children who were securely attached as infants tended to have good self-esteem,[27] experience less depression and anxiety,[28] and develop the ability to have happy, healthy and lasting relationships as adults.[29]

The good news for us as parents is that whether we are in the season of toddler tantrums or teenage traumas, and whether we are parenting together or alone, we are the biggest influence on our children's lives. The family arena is where many of our children's anxieties and fears will play out, but it is also the place where, as parents, we have the opportunity to sow in them the seeds of emotional resilience and wellbeing.

24 John Bowlby et al., 'The effects of mother-child separation: A follow-up study', *British Journal of Media Psychology*, vol.29, no.2, 1956, pp11–247, pubmed.ncbi.gov.
25 Saul McLeod, 'Attachment Theory', *Psychology Today*, 5 February 2017, simplypsychology.org.
26 'Neglect', *Center on the Developing Child: Harvard University*, developingchild. harvard.edu.
27 Chia-heui Wu, 'The Relationship Between Attachment Style and Self-concept Clarity: the mediation effect of self-esteem', *Personality and Individual Differences*, vol.47, no.1, July 2009, pp42–46, pubmed.ncbi.gov.
28 Anouk Spruit et al., 'The Relation Between Attachment and Depression in Children and Adolescents: A Multilevel Meta-Analysis', *Clinical Child and Family Psychology Review*, vol.23, March 2020, pp54–69, pubmed.ncbi.gov.
29 Samantha Rodman, 'How Childhood Attachment Styles Influence Your Adult Relationships', *The Talk Space Voice*, 17 September 2018, talkspace.com.

'Hey, stop fighting. This is a happy house.
One of you start laughing.'

ACTION POINTS

Family matters

- *Tell family stories.* When we tell stories about who we are, it cements our sense of belonging, builds self-esteem and has a positive impact on emotional wellbeing. Tell (and re-tell) your children the story of how you met your partner, ask grandparents to tell stories about your and their childhoods, and talk with your children about their early years.

- *Set up regular routines.* Routines build emotional wellbeing and resilience in children because they create safety and security. While we don't have to stick rigidly to a certain framework, consider the benefits to your family of routines such as set times for getting up, going to bed and meals.

- *Laugh together.* Fun and laughter can actually change our brain chemistry to positively influence our emotional wellbeing. Laughter enhances our intake of oxygen, increases the feel-good endorphins released in our brains, strengthens our immune systems, helps to reduce physical feelings of worry and stress, and improves our mood. Watch funny films together, share memes, and make up 'inside' family jokes to build the sense of belonging to a group.

- *Create family rituals.* Develop family traditions – for example, movie nights on a Friday, pancakes on Christmas morning, always going camping on a particular bank holiday weekend, or special rituals or activities on birthdays. It doesn't matter what the traditions are, but they are important to wellbeing because they reinforce belonging, identity and safety.

- *Celebrate as a family as often as possible.* It may seem obvious, but a happy family atmosphere engenders wellbeing. As a family, make it a habit to celebrate things both big and small – for example, the first day of school, the start of the school holidays, getting a holiday job, finding something that was lost. The celebrations don't have to be expensive – going to the park together, having an ice cream at a local beauty spot, or having a no homework night can still be a special occasion.

- *Monitor your child's media use, both the content and the amount of time spent on screens.* Be aware of how much time they are spending on screens and who they might be interacting with on social media and online games, and put in appropriate internet filters and controls.

ACTIVITY

Begin a family fun book in which you record the funny things your children said when they were young and the jokes or events that made you laugh. You could even insert their funny drawings and hilarious photos. Get it out and read it often.

'I'm worried about our baby. He's so negative –
crying about EVERYTHING.'

CHAPTER 3

WHAT ARE YOU THINKING?

Leyla sighed as she came downstairs. She'd hoped that today would be different, that Mackenzie would have started to settle after all the disruption of starting his first term of secondary school. He had come home and gone straight to his room; she suspected he'd been crying. She thought about parents' evening last night, admittedly it was easier to be there now it was online, but also somehow more abrupt. She thought how negative the art teacher had been to him, wincing as she remembered some of the words he had used to describe Mackenzie's efforts: 'lacking creativity', 'poor', 'disappointing'. It was true that Mackenzie struggled academically, and Leyla would be the first to admit he wasn't the most studious of pupils, but she knew he'd tried really hard on this project. Surely the teacher hadn't needed to be quite so down on him? Although some of the other subject teachers had been more encouraging, Mackenzie's thoughts now seemed to be spiralling downwards again. She'd tried to jolly him out of it many times, trying to get him to be more positive, but it seemed to be a lost cause.

As parents, it's not easy to hear our child express negative thoughts or see them get stuck in feelings of insignificance, sadness or rejection. We all have an 'inner voice' – a story playing inside our minds. It's as if we put on a pair of glasses every morning that are either rose-tinted or a dull grey, and they inform our thinking. Researchers say that it's easier for our brains to dwell more on negative thoughts and feelings than on positive ones – psychologists call it 'negativity bias'. Not only do negative events and experiences imprint on our brains more quickly than positive ones, they also linger longer. According to psychologist Dr Rick Hansen, the amygdala (what he calls the 'alarm bell' of the brain) uses two-thirds of its neurons to look for bad news.[30] Once the alarm sounds, these negative events and experiences are quickly stored in the memory. On the other hand, positive events and experiences need to be held in awareness for over ten seconds to transfer from short to long-term storage.

Research also shows that negativity bias is exaggerated in children. One study found that when asked to 'rate' the emotions of neutral facial expressions, children tended to assume that these neutral expressions were actually angry.[31] Teenagers also tend towards negativity. The teenage brain is rapidly changing, especially in relation to core issues such as friendship, body image and identity, and one of the by-products is that it triggers negative thoughts and emotions more easily than an adult brain. When triggered, these emotions are much more overwhelming for them and harder to ignore.

The difference that a negative and positive attitude makes to our emotional wellbeing is significant. At the youth club, 16-year-old Seth overhears some of his year group talking about forming a band. He is a talented drummer and being in a band has always been his

30 Margaret Jaworski, 'What is the negativity bias? How can you overcome it?', *Psycom*, 19 February 2020, psycom.net.
31 Hilary A. Marusak et al., 'Convergent behavioral and corticolimbic connectivity evidence of a negativity bias in children and adolescents', *Social Cognitive and Affective Neuroscience*, vol.12, no.4, April 2017, pp517–525.

dream. On the way home, he begins thinking about how great it would be if he could be a part of it, but then his inner voice takes over: 'Even if they need a drummer, they won't want me. They all live over the other side of town. Anyway, I'm not good enough.' Over the next few days, these negative thoughts loop over and over in Seth's mind, causing the stress chemical cortisol to be released in his brain.

Cortisol is released as part of the body's fight or flight response to a stressful situation, stimulating reactions that prepare us either to stay and fight the challenge or escape to safety. It's a brilliant survival mechanism – just what we need if we are faced with a grizzly bear or an out of control number one bus. But the problem is that our bodies can't tell the difference between a genuine danger and a false alarm. Without a genuine danger to deal with, cortisol will build up in our system, triggering yet more stress and anxious thoughts.[32]

Leah and Maria are doing what they love best – spending Saturday afternoon in town shopping. They squeeze into the changing room together to try on jeans and a top. The soft lighting and changing room mirror make them look great, and they both take a selfie. Later that evening, they post the pictures on social media. They both gets lots of likes. Then a comment comes about Maria's picture saying that she'd better do something about her tummy. Maria laughs to herself and takes a closer look at her photo: 'Hmmm, maybe they're right … too many doughnuts on the way home from school.' In only a few seconds, though, her thoughts have moved on in a different direction: 'It's brilliant that this top was in the sale – it looks really good on me.'

Just as Maria is looking at her photo and feeling upbeat about her new top, Leah is heading to bed and sneaking a look at her phone. She sees that someone has commented that she has 'scrawny arms'. She can't get it out of her mind and pretty soon her thoughts are in freefall, her inner voice giving her a running commentary on her

32 'Understanding the stress response', *Harvard Health Publishing: Harvard Medical School*, March 2011, health.harvard.edu.

looks: 'My arms are really scrawny. I don't work out enough and I'll never have a good body. I'm so ugly.' Suddenly, after a fun day trying on clothes with her friend, the power of her negative thinking has taken the joy away completely. Now she feels bad about herself and demoralized.

The two friends think in very different ways; Maria has a positive outlook on life, but Leah's attitude shows an underlying negativity bias. But even if we and our children have a tendency to negative thinking, the good news is that it's possible to train our brains to think more positively. Scientists used to believe that the brain's ability to change and grow – its 'plasticity' – was only possible in early childhood. After this, the brain's thought patterns became fixed. However, research has shown that the brain continues to change throughout our lives,[33] and it can be trained to be more emotionally resilient.[34]

The brain is a pattern-seeking device, so when the neurons in our brains are stimulated to work in a particular pattern, it's faster for the same patterns to be followed in the future.[35] The next time we do the activity, we will therefore find it easier. The time after that, it will be easier still, and so on. Our brains aren't fixed, and through practice we can build stronger and more positive neural pathways.

Imagine that you are trying to walk across an overgrown field. You have to fight your way through tall grasses, ferns, weeds and brambles. It's hard work, but you make it. The next day, because you flattened some of the undergrowth the day before, the field is a little easier to cross. The following day it's easier still. Eventually, by walking over it again and again, you make a clear, wide, path.

33 Amanda E. Guyer et al., 'Opportunities for Neurodevelopmental Plasticity From Infancy Through Early Adulthood', *Child Development*, vol.89, no.3, May – June 2018, pp687–697.
34 Debbie Hampton, 'The Neuroscience of Building a Resilient Brain', *The Best Brain Possible*, 5 August 2018, thebestbrainpossible.com.
35 Judy Willis, 'What Brain Research Suggests for Teaching Reading Strategies', *The Educational Forum*, vol.73, no.4, 16 September 2009, pp333–346.

'Dad, maybe you could re-frame the situation
and challenge your negativity?'

In the same way, our thought processes build pathways in our brains. If we constantly have negative thoughts, the negative pathways become well used, and when faced with the option of a clear path or fighting through the undergrowth, our brain will choose the easiest route. This process means that we have the opportunity to help our children develop a positive mindset by encouraging them to choose positive rather than negative thoughts. At first it's hard work, but as they choose to stop thinking negative thoughts their neural pathways will gradually rewire and positive pathways will take over to become the motorways of their brain.

According to the positive psychology researcher Barbara Fredrickson, positive thinking is important because it broadens our sense of possibility and opens our mind, allowing us to build new skills and become more resilient. Fredrickson recommends overcoming the bias we have towards negativity by developing a 3:1 ratio of positive to negative thoughts.[36] As parents, we can seek to nurture this balance of positivity in our children by encouraging them not to take on board negative thoughts about things, but to find positive things to think about instead that make them feel good and build their self-esteem.

One caveat: while we want to help our children develop a positive outlook on life, this isn't about pretending everything in the garden is rosy when it clearly isn't. Expecting them to be deliriously happy 24/7 isn't realistic or helpful for their emotional wellbeing as it's important to have both positive and negative emotions. If we didn't feel sad, we wouldn't have empathy; and if we didn't feel guilt or shame, we wouldn't have a moral compass. Parents will know very well that as well as being easily triggered, their teenagers' emotions often swing from one extreme to another. Learning how to manage these extremes, including lifting their mood when the world seems at an end, is one of the challenges of teenage life.

36 Barbara L. Fredrickson, *Positivity: Top-Notch Research Reveals the 3 to 1 Ratio That Will Change Your Life* (Harmony, 2009).

Psychologist Svend Brinkmann explains that happiness is simply not the appropriate response to many situations in life, and the pressure to always think positively 'has turned happiness into a duty and a burden.'[37] In fact, research indicates that emotional avoidance (not facing up to negative feelings) is one of the main causes of many psychological issues.[38] So while encouraging positive thinking, we need also to help our children recognize and accept some negative emotions and process them in a healthy way.

Catch, challenge, change

A friend of mine has a useful framework to help children realize that just because they are thinking something it doesn't necessarily make it true. He encourages his children first to *catch* their thought, next to *challenge* the truth of it, and then to *change* that thought to a more positive one.

Fifteen-year-old Maggie hadn't slept well, her mind buzzing as she checked her phone throughout the night. A few days earlier, she'd confided in her friend Robyn about her feelings for Finley. Tall, dark and athletic, Finley was in the year above. They'd met a few weeks before in the after-school drama club and Maggie was smitten. She was the youngest in her year and not as sophisticated as her friends, and she knew she probably didn't stand a chance, but Robyn had persuaded her to text him to see if he'd like to meet up. She'd taken a few attempts to work out what she wanted to say, but eventually she composed the message and pressed send. Within seconds, the three little dots came up to indicate he was replying ... her heart missed a beat. But just as quickly as they'd come, the dots disappeared and, since then, nothing.

37 Olivia Goldhill, '"Positive thinking" has turned happiness into a duty and a burden, says a Danish psychologist', *Quartz*, 4 March 2017, qz.com.
38 Noam Shpancer, 'Emotional Acceptance: Why Feeling Bad is Good', *Psychology Today*, 8 September 2010, psychologytoday.com.

As Maggie turned the corner on the way to school next morning she noticed a group of friends chatting by the gate and started to cross the road to say *hi* when one of them spotted her. Suddenly, everyone stopped talking and looked at her. Then, after an awkward pause, one of them started to laugh. Maggie blushed, turned and hurried into school. Heading straight for the changing rooms, she ran in and locked the door behind her, her thoughts racing. Robyn must have told them about her text to Finley and now they were all laughing at her. She'd never felt so embarrassed and foolish. How on earth could she ever face them again – let alone face Finley? The fact he hadn't even bothered to reply obviously meant he thought she was ugly. She should have known better. Why would anyone want to go out with someone in the year below with short legs, a big nose and braces on her teeth? If only she was pretty.

Our brains are wired to help us survive and at 8.55am that morning Maggie's brain was working overtime with negative thoughts, trying to make sense of the situation. But there could have been any number of explanations for what had happened. Her friends could have been laughing about something that was nothing to do with her and there could be other reasons why Finley hadn't replied. While her interpretation of the events *may* have been correct, it certainly wasn't the only one.

If Maggie had learnt to *catch*, *challenge* and *change* her negative thoughts, she could have avoided the miserable few days that followed. By putting the events under the microscope of what she actually knew for sure was true, she could have realized she was making a negative assumption and changed this to include more positive interpretations. And if the worst explanation did turn out to be true, she could have chosen not to allow her thoughts to escalate and found ways of dealing with the situation.

ACTION POINTS

What Are You Thinking?

- *Surround your children with positive people.* This doesn't mean that we can never let them near those who tend to see the glass as half-empty, but bear in mind that the people we spend time with have a big influence on us; if our children are among positive and happy people, this will affect how they perceive things too.

- *Helping others.* The saying that it is more blessed to give than to receive applies to acts of kindness too. Encouraging our children to help others – giving tips to a younger sibling about their homework, cutting an elderly neighbour's grass for them, raising money for charity – will help them feel good about themselves and give them a sense of purpose.

- *Create a family Wow Journal.* This is a book in which you and your children can record 'wow' moments in your everyday lives – perhaps a nice thing that someone did, something funny or extraordinary that happened, or something they find awesome or beautiful. Get them to record these moments with drawings, photos or written descriptions.

- *Blue to True thinking.* This is another way of helping your children to catch, challenge and change negative thoughts:
  1. Get them to recognize any 'blue' thoughts – for example, thinking negatively about themselves or catastrophizing.
  2. Ask them to replace these thoughts with 'true' thoughts about themselves or the situation.
  3. Encourage them to 'remember' these true thoughts by keeping a list of them in a notebook or on their phone to look at when the blue thoughts return.

- *Ask your child what they would say to their friend.* Getting them to think about the question 'What would you say to a friend if they were in your situation?' can be an effective way to help them think more positively about themselves.

- *Encourage an attitude of gratitude.* Studies show that counting our blessings improves psychological, emotional, and physical wellbeing. As a family, show your appreciation to people who have helped or been kind to you. Sending a homemade card or text message, or baking a cake will not only lift the recipient's spirits but make your children feel good as well.

- *Practice positive thinking.* Rather than asking 'How was your day?', say 'Tell me one *good* thing from your day.' They can then share any challenges too.

ACTIVITY

1. Ask everyone in the family to name three things that went well today – however big or small. For example, winning a football game, having a favourite pudding for lunch, dealing well with a difficult friend.

2. Then say why it happened. For example, 'We won the game because we practised hard', 'My favourite pudding was on the school menu today' or 'I managed to calm my friend down before he got into trouble.'

3. Now, if you still have everyone's attention, encourage them to name what character strengths were used in that situation. For example, kindness, perseverance, gratitude, empathy. (Younger children may, of course, need help with this.)

'Can we watch it later, Dad?
I need to alphabetize my books.'

CHAPTER 4

WHAT DOES SUCCESS LOOK LIKE?

Rachel closed her bedroom door and turned on her laptop; it seemed to take an eternity to connect. Her heart was racing, her mouth was dry and she had a knot in her stomach. The email was in her inbox, just waiting to be opened. One click, and the agony would be over – she'd know if she'd done enough to get the grades for her university place. At that moment, it felt like her whole future hung in the balance.

Every year, scenes like this are played out in homes across the world as children receive news of the final school exam results that will determine the course of their future. And for children whose education has been disrupted by the pandemic and whose final exams have been cancelled there is the additional stress of not knowing what metrics will be used for giving them their grades. Worries about exams are right up there among the things that keep teenagers up at night. And no wonder. When I was at school, we had two lots of public exams and that was it. So, in terms of stress, there were two main occasions when our bodies geared up with the 'fight or flight' chemicals needed to motivate us to focus and then calm down again. For today's children it's a different story. In an education system focussed on targets and rankings, they are assessed almost as soon as they can walk; private nurseries have entrance exams and even interviews, and primary school pupils sitting SATs don't take long to realize that the tests are measuring not just where the school comes in the league table but also where they come in the class order. As they move to secondary school, the pressure increases with frequent important tests and less recovery time in between. And this pressure continues into further education. University applications now have to read like CVs. As well as getting top grades, it seems that young people are expected to have zip-wired across the Victoria Falls, led a team out of the Amazon jungle and run a small business enterprise from their bedroom!

Add to this toxic mix the pressure of media publicity. If Rachel cares to turn on breakfast TV, she will be hijacked with pictures of ecstatic teenagers (girls in the main) whooping with delight and waving envelopes containing that coveted cluster of As and with them a golden ticket to their university of choice.

Maybe it's no surprise then to find that exam stress and anxiety is overwhelming our young people. In a national survey of school leaders and governors in 2017, 79% saw an increase in anxiety and panic attacks among pupils.[39] In the same year, Childline reported delivering 3,000 counselling sessions on exam stress – an increase of over 11% on the previous year.[40] And this pressure is being felt by the 'A-grade, form-captain, 1st team hockey, grade 8 piano' students whose parents micromanage their progress just as much as those who, for whatever reason, aren't ever going to stand on the podium of academic success. Commenting on this tragedy, parenting journalist and author Tanith Carey writes:

39 'State of Education: Survey Report 2017', *The Key*, 2017, stateofed.thekeyssupport.com.
40 Sophie Gallagher, 'Exam Stress Is Causing Thousands Of UK Children To Require Counselling, Says Childline', *Huffington Post,* 12 May 2017, huffingtonpost.co.uk.

At one end of the scale, high-stakes testing is turbo-charging an elite class of alpha children who have been on the hamster wheel from the moment of birth. At the other, it is alienating a generation of children who have been branded as failures early on because they never got the same level of parental investment.[41]

The good news is that there is much we can do as parents to help our children build an emotional buffer against overwhelming anxiety about school and exams. How we approach this looks slightly different depending on where our children are on the bell curve of academic achievement.

Parenting high achievers

Most of us as parents would give our right arm to have a child who turns down a night out in town to complete their physics homework, whose teachers' comments leave us basking in the aura of a warm glow at parents' evening, and who walks away with enough class awards to sink the *Titanic*. A child like that ticks all the boxes in society's definition of success – and if we are honest, those ticked boxes don't look too bad on *our* report card as parents either. But if we scratch beneath the surface, there's sometimes a different story. While some children are natural rule-followers and do their homework when it's set, other high-achieving children are driven by perfectionism and self-criticism and are susceptible to debilitating worry. Believing that their worth is based on their exam results, although it may look on paper as if they are doing well, many are actually feeling overwhelmed.

This scenario seems to be particularly the case for girls. Stanford psychologist Carol Dweck writes: 'If life were one long grade school,

---

41 Tanith Carey, *Taming the Tiger Parent: How to put your child's well-being first in a competitive world* (Robinson, 2014), p11.

girls would rule the world.'[42] The reason is that school generally offers the kind of structured environment where girls tend to thrive – lessons where you put your hand up to speak, you are praised for a right answer, and legible handwriting and homework handed in on time is a priority. The problem is that these behaviours can backfire. Needing to get everything right can lead to crippling perfectionism, fear of failure, and a lack of resilience in the face of challenge – characteristics which are, in any case, generally more common in girls than boys.

As parents, we can check whether our expectations of our children, unintentionally or not, are adding fuel to the fire. When a group of secondary school children were interviewed about their wellbeing, many spoke passionately about the pressure for academic success they felt their parents put them under. Comments such as 'My parents get quite annoyed if I don't get a good mark in something. It does put a lot of stress on me' and 'My family doesn't accept failures' were not uncommon.[43]

A recent study of students in a socially advantaged setting looked at how their parents' values affected their wellbeing. They found that children with parents who were less focused on their academic achievement had higher self-worth, lower psychological symptoms and actually did better at school.[44] While we don't want to throw the baby out with the bathwater (encouraging our children's learning is important!), sometimes the best thing we can do for our high-achieving children is to take our foot off the pedal and help them do the same. It's easier said than done, but we need to encourage them to let go of their perfectionist standards and see downtime as an integral part of academic success.

42 Carol Dweck and Rachel Simmons, 'Why do women fail?', *CNN*, 30 July 2014, edition.cnn.com.

43 Rachel Rosen, 'The Perfect Generation: Is the internet undermining young people's mental health?', *Parentzone*, 17 March 2016, parentzone.org.uk.

44 Lucia Ciciolla et al., 'When Mothers and Fathers Are Seen as Disproportionately Valuing Achievements: Implications for Adjustment Among Upper Middle Class Youth', *Journal of Youth & Adolescence*, vol.46, 2017, pp1057–1075.

Ali, who is mum to 16-year-old Sophie, comments:

'Sophie has always been keen to do well at school and has worked hard. But while a meltdown over a smudge in her maths book or a crossing out in her English book when she was 11 was easy to deal with, now mistakes or imperfections are more difficult to handle. She has been working late into the night, skipping meals and not seeing friends, and her total focus has been on getting top grades. We decided this wasn't good for her and have encouraged her to try to take regular breaks, see friends at least once during the week, and join us in some family time together. We also chatted about how, while her exams were important, her emotional health and the kind of person she was becoming is what really matters. It wasn't an easy conversation, but urging her to slow down a bit does seem to have taken off the pressure and helped her get a better perspective.'

In Sophie's case, she has gained a more realistic perspective, although she is still motivated by her inner perfectionist. For other perfectionist or high-achieving children, the next stage is procrastination. They see a downgrade for late work, or even not showing up to school at all, as being preferable to bad work. For their parents, this crisis feels as if it has come out of a bright blue sky, but the more likely scenario is that their child's anxious feelings have been building up for some time and have now become overwhelming.

I recently had the privilege of catching up with Zac, who is now a young adult but struggled with the pressure of school. In the first few years of secondary school he did well academically and was usually top of the class. His parents often talked matter-of-factly about the time when he'd go to university and the subject he'd like to read there. One term, when Zac's chemistry marks dropped slightly, his father appointed a tutor to make sure that he was soon achieving high marks again. When the time came for him to choose his subject options, Zac remembers feeling under enormous stress. Waking up one morning, he knew something was different. He said, 'It was as if someone had flicked a switch. I couldn't face going to school.'

That moment ushered in days at a time when Zac hardly left his bedroom, let alone the house. He felt numb and described feeling as if he was living in a bubble. His parents, teachers, social workers and health professionals all tried to help and cajole him back to his studies without success. I later chatted to Zac's parents. Their story mirrored his account as they recalled how, after never previously missing school, he'd started to have the odd day off, saying he was unwell, and this had quickly snowballed into him refusing to leave the house. His dad, Pete, commented, 'We might have seen it coming if we'd known what to look for, but we didn't. We thought it was a phase and that things would get better. Our waking thought every day was about how to get Zac to school.'

Kate, Zac's mum, remembers the school attendance officer coming to the house and asking her, 'What does "getting better" look like for Zac?' Her reply had been, 'Him attending school.' Both parents now agree that they'd been unable to see the wood for the trees. Kate said, 'I've often looked back on my answer to that question and I now realize that a better response would have been simply, "For Zac not to feel stressed and to be able to participate in life."'

They had previously bought a PlayStation for Zac, a reward for doing well in his music at school, and he stayed in his room for hours at a time playing FIFA. Pete told me:

'It was as if I had tunnel vision. I thought his gaming was getting in the way of his being at school and that if I stopped him doing that, all would be well. I tried every tactic possible. I removed the controllers and then the hard drive – all to no avail. It seemed only to increase the pressure he felt and resulted in him shutting his bedroom door for days on end. I can (almost) see the funny side of it now, but I was so desperate to get him out of his room that I got a screwdriver and removed the bedroom door. Crazy, I know! He simply moved into a tent in the garden. What we didn't understand was that his bedroom was his 'safe place' – his place away from the pressures. Instead of

seeing it as an act of defiance, I should have come alongside him and protected that space.'

The turning point for the family came when Kate and Pete decided that Zac's emotional wellbeing was more important than him returning to school to do his exams. They stood back and took the pressure off him by giving him a choice whether to go back to school or not (and making it clear that they would be happy whatever he decided).

In chatting to Kate and Pete, I found their honesty and vulnerability refreshing. One of the keys to helping Zac was their ability to admit where they'd got things wrong. They were wise enough to put their preconceived ideas aside and ask what path in life was best for him. What were his strengths and his passions? They didn't have to look far to find the answer: cycling. Before his anxiety had overtaken him, he'd loved spending every spare moment of his time on his bike and, encouraged by his parents, he applied for a job in a local bike shop. Zac told me: 'I've been working there for a couple of years now, and it's changed everything. I'm doing what I love and the pressure has gone.' He still struggles with perfectionism but having something that he truly enjoys doing and without the external stresses, he finds he is able to manage this well.

A group of secondary school teachers commented that students were often reluctant to talk to their parents for fear of upsetting them or letting them down, and they frequently opened up to staff instead. One head teacher said, 'This school sees intense pressure on young people today to be "the perfect generation", making them less willing to admit they need help.'[45]

As parents, of course we'll want our children to work hard and fulfil their potential, but it is a tragedy if they interpret this as us setting the bar so high that they worry about not living up to our expectations and don't feel they can talk to us if they are struggling.

45 Rachel Rosen, 'The Perfect Generation'.

Finding times to regularly connect with our children and keep communication lines open is vital. They need to know that they can always come to us whatever the issue.

Parenting the underperformers

Not all young people are suited to a life in the ivory towers of academia, and many find the well-trodden route of A-levels and university stressful. I often felt between a rock and a hard place with my own children. On one hand, at times I wanted to give them a proverbial kick up the backside when I knew they needed it (for example, to open their geography textbook in the first place) and on the other, I didn't want to put pressure on them and give them the message that academic success was everything. A parent's nagging or encouraging may perhaps edge a D to a C; however, our approach may need a paradigm shift. Author and parenting expert Dr John Duffy writes:

> It's ... important that we meet our kids where they are and appreciate the strengths they currently have, even if they are not measured on an attendance sheet or on a report card. So if your child is an aspiring rapper ... give their music a listen and provide them some feedback. If they are Insta-fabulous (as one of my clients has deemed herself), check out her social media feeds. You might be surprised there. Be open to that. You may have a budding dancer on your hands ... Your child's strengths may not be what you would have chosen, but they come by them honestly. We are missing a mighty parenting opportunity, and driving depression and anxiety, if we dismiss these passions and strengths as folly, worthless or unacceptable. There's a chance to relieve anxiety here and build self-worth.[46]

This isn't about hanging up our boots and resigning ourselves to our child doing nothing. They may argue otherwise, but deep down

---

46 John Duffy, *Parenting the New Teen in the Age of Anxiety: A Complete Guide to Your Child's Stressed, Depressed, Expanded, Amazing Adolescence* (Mango, 2019), p98.

they want to thrive, and as their parents we want them to fulfil their potential. But if we are constantly on their backs, working harder for their achievements than they are, we may need to press the reset button and try a different approach. Fatima felt at her wits' end with her teenage son's reluctance to do any schoolwork. She said:

> '*My nagging was just making things worse and making us both anxious. Instead of encouraging him to work, it resulted in him downing tools altogether. Of course his schoolwork was important, and I wanted him to fulfil his potential, but when I took a step back I realized that our relationship and his emotional health were more important than his test results. I decided I would have one last chat with him, lay it on the line, and then leave it up to him and the school. While I can't say everything changed with regard to schoolwork, without my criticising and cajoling him 24/7 he certainly became less anxious and our relationship improved no end, which is what really mattered.*'

Her experience is backed up by psychologist Robert Myers who says that nagging weakens the parent-child bond: 'The more you nag, the less they hear.'[47] It creates resentment and can make them feel controlled and manipulated.

It is also important to recognize developmental differences, especially in relation to younger, primary-aged children. Although many schools focus on academic milestones, academic gifting is not the whole story. Other abilities such as concentration and impulse control are key in enabling our children to perform well. Another significant factor, at least until the end of Key Stage One, is their age in the school year. Two of my boys have birthdays in the first week of September and were the oldest in the year, and the difference between their stamina and stage of development with that of their younger friends born in the last week of August was marked.

47 Robert Myers, '7 Reasons Why Nagging Doesn't Work', *Empowering Parents*, empoweringparents.com.

At our Care for the Family events we often remind parents: 'Don't read your children's school reports at half time.' Children develop at different rates and some don't grow into their ability until secondary school, but by then they may have labelled themselves as 'naughty', 'stupid' or 'clumsy', or simply have opted out. Understanding this as parents means that we can avoid labelling our children, take a step back and look behind issues like poor behaviour to see if frustration might in fact be part of the problem.

Wellness as the cornerstone of success

While teachers are my heroes and school results are important, they are not the only metric of ability or success in life. In fact, our narrow definition of success is a significant contributor to the anxiety that many young people are feeling. As parents, we want our children to do well, so that they have as many opportunities open to them as possible, but if we aren't careful we can put them into a very small box where there is no room for creativity, individuality or exploration. This does nothing for the self-esteem of the child who doesn't fit into that box, and their unique gifts and talents can be overlooked.

It's natural for parents to have hopes and ambitions for their children, so it can be challenging to choose to put those aside in preference to the dreams they have for themselves. But important as their English, maths or science GCSEs and A-levels are, the most important A* is in emotional health. Being open to redefining success in the cause of our children's wellbeing is the hallmark of a wise parent.

ACTION POINTS

What Does Success Look Like?

- *Celebrate effort.* Agree that you'll take a teenager who has worked hard for their exams out for a treat on the day of their last exam rather than on results day.

- *Look out for signs that your child is being overstretched.* If their grades start falling, they seem to be tired a lot, or they are displaying other signs of stress, consider carefully what is being expected of them and whether it is too much.

- *Praise character qualities.* 'I was so proud of you last night helping Olivia get home from the party. It shows how thoughtful and caring you are.' Praise for character is powerful and affirming; it gives our children the message that who they are is more important than what they achieve, and it builds self-esteem.

- *Simplify their lives – even just for the short term.* If your child is anxious and stressed it may be helpful to take the pressure off them by cutting down on their activities. Make sure, though, that you don't stop them from doing things that are uplifting and that they enjoy.

- *Colour code the diary.* Get your children to colour code each activity of their week. For example, red for something exhausting or unenjoyable (a maximum of one per day); orange for a neutral activity which they neither enjoy or dislike; and green for something enjoyable and restorative (at least one per day). This is a great way to help them manage their time, get to know themselves, and learn not to overload their days.

ACTIVITY

In exam time:

1. Help your teenagers work out how they study best (in their room or at the kitchen table; on their own or with others; with or without music) and then help them control their environment accordingly. If they need peace and quiet, make a plan for keeping younger siblings out of the way.

2. Be flexible about household jobs. Don't worry about untidy bedrooms – they can wait.

3. Be understanding of unusual moodiness.

4. Arrange some downtime. Sit down with your teenager and brainstorm some fun things they might like to do which will give them a break and keep things in perspective. Balance study time by offering to go out with them for a short burst of activity and some fresh air.

5. Help work out how they learn best – for example, are they a visual learner or an audio learner? Make a revision timetable together and encourage them to stick to it.

6. Be a calm, non-anxious presence around them. If you're not worried about their exams, it will help them not to catastrophise too.

7. Keep the fridge full. When working hard, we need to keep up our energy and so we crave sugar, but body and diet-conscious teenagers may find this a problem. Help them by making sure there are plenty of healthy snacks available.

8. If you work outside the home, remember that teenagers sometimes have trouble taking care of themselves when they have a lot on. Encourage regular bedtimes, eating and exercise routines.

ZIP IT

'Only two more marks and you'd have got an A*! What went wrong?'

'If we can be anything we want, how come
you chose a job you hate?'

CHAPTER 5

IT'S OK TO BE ORDINARY

With four children, I have lost count of the number of junior school sports days I have attended over the years. Looking back, the one constant was the reliability of the British weather to disappoint. As the day approached, settled sunny days would give way to menacing grey clouds and, even worse, sub-zero temperatures. Undeterred by this, serried ranks of eager parents, grandparents and carers would cheer their children on as they threw beanbags, balanced eggs on spoons, jumped in sacks, spun hoops, and ran in the sprint final.

At the end of the morning, every child would be given a Star Certificate – an award for joining in. Whereas my own sports days had featured gold, silver and bronze medals and podium presentations, the message now was very clear: 'Everyone's a winner!' Although some children were perfectly happy with their certificates – giving them pride of place on their bedroom wall for a few weeks at least – I often felt sorry for the children who might not shine academically but were gifted at sports. They would never have the satisfaction of being in the 'red set' (a classification that was a mystery to parents but obviously understood by all the children to mean 'top set') for reading, yet they were denied the chance of a medal on sports day – all in the cause of not damaging everyone else's self-esteem.

The self-esteem movement that began in the 1970s rested on the belief that high self-esteem led to positive mental wellbeing and low self-esteem resulted in poor emotional health. On that premise, it's difficult to argue with the logic: children's mental wellbeing depends on their having good self-esteem and good self-esteem depends on their receiving praise, so praise is paramount. The result of this principle is perhaps predictable – we are so anxious not to damage children's confidence that we imply that they are good at everything. All must have prizes. We tell our children they are geniuses in the making – budding J.K. Rowlings, Harry Kanes, or Elon Musks – and for the avoidance of doubt we buy Babygros, T-shirts, hoodies and bumper stickers to reinforce the message.

I confess to falling into this trap when organizing our children's birthday parties (although I defy any parent to do otherwise when managing a living room full of sugar-fuelled, overexcited 6-year-olds). I would ensure there was exactly the same number of layers of wrapping paper for the game of pass-the-parcel as there were guests at the party, the music orchestrated with everyone mysteriously getting a turn. The final prize was a bag of sweets for the winner to share – because, of course, 'Everyone's a winner.'

In seeking to answer important questions about worth and significance, the self-esteem movement began with good intentions, but the current state of our children's wellbeing perhaps sheds light on the fact that building self-esteem by heaping praise on them for everything they turn their hands to is not the silver bullet that was hoped for.

I am a natural encourager and have unashamedly been our children's biggest cheerleader. Pre-school paintings would be Blu-Tacked to the fridge and given accolades worthy of the Tate Britain. Poems were hailed as signs of budding Laureates. Victory laps of the garden and podium ceremonies on the steps celebrated goals scored. And three-Michelin-star reviews of chocolate crispy cakes gave even Nigella a run for her money. But in the same way that harsh criticism can damage our children's fragile sense of wellbeing, the truth is that overpraising them also does them no favours.

Of course, giving them praise and encouragement is important, but the key is *how* we praise. Rather than showering them with applause for anything and everything, they respond best when praise is specific and they have done something to earn it.

Jack's football team had had a streak of wins and, to their delight, found themselves in the end of season league final. The match was talked up for weeks and in corners of the playground tactics were discussed in hushed tones. On the big day, Jack's mum joined the other parents on the sidelines to cheer the team on. It was a tough match, but they held their own, and for most of the second half they were winning 3-2. Then with one minute to go, the opposition scored. With the score still a tie after extra time, the players now faced a penalty shoot-out – a tough enough gig for grown men in the Premier League let alone a team of impressionable 8-year-olds. As Jack stepped up to take the final penalty, he felt the weight of the world on his shoulders. It was all down to him. The goal looked enormous – how could he miss? His mother's heart was in her mouth as she saw her son step forward and kick the ball with confidence, then watched it sail over the goal and into the field beyond.

On the way home, Jack was inconsolable and everything in her wanted to stop him hurting. Phrases like 'You played brilliantly', 'That was such a great game', and 'Your team were the best' were on the tip of her tongue. But Jack's mum was wise. She knew that when we overpraise our children they see through it – it doesn't ring true. So she tried another tactic. 'Jack, I know it was disappointing to lose, but I loved the fact you were brave enough to take that final penalty. I was proud of you.'

When our children do well, of course we need to praise their achievement. But it's much more important to praise character, attitude and effort. Whilst we may get away with overpraising them when they are little, it sets the bar high and leads to their believing that their worth lies solely in what they achieve and not in who they are. Having good self-esteem is not about knowing you are perfect but about knowing you are good enough.

Thousands of hopeful stars braving mile-long queues to audition for *The X Factor* or sending in their videos and CVs to the producers of *The Apprentice* are evidence of the fact that a generation of young people have been duped into believing they are extraordinary. Of course, every single one of us is unique and has the potential to develop skills and talents, but the reality is that only a minority are destined for stardom.

An anxious mum recently reached out for some advice:

> *'My daughter, aged 10, wants to be a pop star when she grows up, but she is a really bad singer – she just can't sing in tune! Earlier this year she asked me if she could try for Britain's Got Talent. I said no, but she went on and on about it until I gave in, just to keep her quiet. I honestly thought there was no chance she'd get through, but I've just found out she's gone and got an audition! Should I take her to it, knowing that she'll be disappointed? I hate the thought of lying to her, but maybe it's best to protect her and not even tell her about the audition. What do I do? Help!'*

While I have a huge amount of sympathy for this mum and every bit of me would want to protect the fragile sensitivities of a 10-year-old, we do our children no favours if we fail to help them develop a realistic view of themselves and of life (and the honest truth is that this mum should probably have dissuaded her daughter from entering in the first place). The belief that 'I have to be extraordinary' is a major driver of anxiety and one of the main factors affecting children's wellbeing. Having been sold the lie that they can be and do anything, is it any wonder that so many young people report feeling depressed and anxious when no one presses the golden buzzer for

'My room is good enough just as it is, OK?'

them? When life itself delivers the verdict that they aren't quite so extraordinary after all?

Our children are growing up in a culture of entitlement where talent shows, TikTok videos and Instagram Reels turn the ordinary into the extraordinary every day of the week. Singing, dancing, cooking, baking and even falling in love have become a national competition, a spectator sport with winners and losers. So perhaps it's no surprise that children feel under pressure to do something special and stand out from the crowd, not just in relation to schoolwork or sports, but in every area of life. The irony, of course, is that the very nature of being extraordinary means it's not possible for everyone.

Our culture's celebration of the high achievers in life has even led to children who are articulate, hardworking, dependable and reliable feeling useless and overlooked. But in real life these are the people who are sought after as friends, colleagues and employees – the people we all want to be on our team.

Our ability to embrace and accept reality, with all its limitations and disappointments, is at the heart of emotional wellbeing. As parents, one of the most important messages we can give our children is that it's OK to be ordinary.

The success of the BBC's adaptation of Sally Rooney's bestselling novel *Normal People* is perhaps an insight into the fact that normality is precisely what young people are secretly yearning for. Whilst the graphic nature of the content means the series isn't recommended viewing for everyone, the surprising thing about its popularity is that there are no scenes of high drama, no cliffhangers, no heart-stopping twists and turns in the plot, but simply the unfolding lives of two Irish teenagers into young adulthood. Unvarnished and real, with moments of joy but also deep regret, misunderstanding and disappointment, it's a story of normal life that is beautifully *ordinary*.

Maybe some of the pressures on young people to be extraordinary come from the fact that culture has framed an 'ordinary' life as dull and unfulfilling. But as parents, we have the opportunity to step in and change that narrative. We can help them recognize that ordinary life is not about settling for a boring second-best; it is about embracing reality, making the most of every opportunity and becoming the best 'me' we can be.

Competition is a fact of life for both adults and children, but our children will deal with it more effectively if it is built on a foundation of healthy self-awareness that enables them to simply give their best. Lucy remembers taking her son Nathan to compete in a school maths championship. Maths had always been his strongest subject, but this competition was at a much higher level than those he'd previously taken part in. For most of the short journey to the school he chattered without pause, a sure sign of his nervousness, rehearsing all his previous competition scores and where he'd made mistakes, the marks his friends had got and the mistakes they'd made, and how much better he could do this time.

Listening to his monologue, Lucy recognised his anxiety. She wanted him to do well of course, but he was only nine! How had he already become so fixated on needing to excel? As they drew up to the school gates, Nathan fell silent and Lucy's mind was racing as she thought of all the things she longed to say to him:

> 'Nathan, calm down. It's not helpful to compare yourself to others. You don't always need to be in the spotlight. You don't have to beat your friends – in fact, life isn't a competition. There are more important things than maths tests. Being kind, looking out for your friends – those sorts of things count far more.'

But as important as it was to give him these messages, she knew that particular moment wasn't the right time. There would be better occasions on which to sow these thoughts in his mind: school runs, meal times, film nights, trips to the park, early morning or late night chats and the many other moments that made up the patchwork of family life. Resolving to make the most of those opportunities, she gave him a friendly fist bump and watched him run up the school steps to face what she anticipated might be another lesson in the classroom of life.

The life-sapping pressures on our children to prove themselves to be special and extraordinary is something that we, as parents, can work hard to lift from their shoulders.

We can help them have a realistic view of themselves, and this means encouraging them to celebrate their strengths and to know and manage their weaknesses.

In his bestselling book *The Boy, The Mole, The Fox and The Horse*,[48] Charlie Mackesy uses a simple story and a series of beautiful ink drawings to convey deep truths about the human heart and things that are really important in life. One of my favourites is his picture of the boy sitting close to the fox with the horse standing nearby.

'What's your best discovery?' asks the mole, looking up at the boy.

'That I'm enough as I am,' the boy replies.

We can help our children make that 'best discovery' for themselves. We want them to know deep down that whatever messages they may hear to the contrary, 'I am enough.' It really is OK to be ordinary.

48 Charlie Mackesy, *The Boy, The Mole, The Fox and The Horse,* (Ebury Press, 2019).

ACTION POINTS

It's OK to be Ordinary

- *Give specific praise.* Instead of a general comment such as 'You're great', praising your children for specific things makes far more of an impact. For example, 'You were very careful building that tower of bricks. Good job!' or 'I was so proud of you last night when our neighbour came round just as you wanted me to play a game with you. You were so patient.'

- *Go big on birthdays.* Birthdays are great for building self-esteem, because they celebrate who you are, not what you've done.

- *Set them up for success.* Challenging our children and giving them something to work towards is important, but it's also helpful to give them opportunities which make them feel confident, comfortable, and where they are sure to be successful.

- *Affirm your child's efforts and good qualities.* Don't limit praise to successes or achievements; recognize their other attributes. For example, 'You were so kind to that new boy in school. Well done!' or 'I can see how hard you tried with that homework.' Encouragement and affirmations that don't depend on any kind of achievement are important for building our children's wellbeing and self-esteem. And they can be even more powerful if they catch us saying something positive about them to someone else.

- *Assign age-appropriate chores.* Psychologists believe that manageable contributions to family life and the community promote self-esteem and problem-solving ability. Whether it's walking the dog, folding the washing or laying the table, it gives a sense of belonging, empowerment and satisfaction at the completion of a task.

- *Help your child discover a passion.* Encourage your child to pursue a hobby, activity or interest that really grabs them – even if it's something that's very different to your own interests. Allowing them to simply be themselves is key to building confidence and a sense of identity.

ACTIVITY

Make a Self-Appreciation Chart for your children. Over the course of a month, ask them to write down one good thing about themselves every day. It doesn't matter how big or small it is – what is important is that they recognize the many things for which they can love and appreciate themselves.

ZIP IT

'Why can't you be more like ...?'

'Please don't cry. I don't cry. Your grandfather
doesn't cry. It's genetic.'

CHAPTER 6

IT'S OK TO BE EMOTIONAL

'Don't be so emotional!' I remember those words being directed at me while I was in a high state of teenage angst about an issue that seemed unbelievably unjust and which (with all the wisdom of a 14-year-old) I considered my parents to have completely misjudged. I'd been given a new coat for my birthday which I was thrilled with, and I wanted to wear it to school, a request they refused. It was the first item of teenage clothing I had possessed, and my desire to show my peers that I could keep up with the best of them had been thwarted. In my adolescent world, it was nothing less than a catastrophe.

Emotions are part of the way our brains are designed. We can't escape them or avoid having them, and they are what makes life feel worth living (and ending). But how we manage our emotions – particularly when they are difficult or painful – is important for our wellbeing.

When I was a student, my hall of residence had a notoriously sensitive smoke alarm. If a piece of toast got singed, the alarm would be activated. Deafening decibels across the surrounding neighbourhood were a minor annoyance at lunchtime, but they became a serious antisocial nuisance in the context of the (more frequent) 2am cooking activities that took place after a night on the town. Psychologist Dr Kate Middleton uses the helpful analogy of emotions such as anxiety being like that smoke alarm – their job is to alert our minds to the fact that something is going on and to trigger a response. They are our brain's way of grabbing our attention and giving us a signal to act.[49]

However, although they are important signals, our emotions are not necessarily truthful or reliable. Like my hall of residence smoke detector, they may be oversensitive. Just because we (or our children) *feel* that we are stupid, clumsy or ... [fill in the blank], it doesn't mean that we are.

As parents, as well as managing our own emotions, we have the added responsibility of helping our children make sense of their feelings. Babies are not delivered as the finished article, and just as children have to learn to walk and talk, responding in a healthy way to our emotions is a skill we need to learn to master.

A baby's first smile is a red-letter day for new parents. After six exhausting weeks of pouring themselves into a new little life with seemingly scant response, this is the first sign of emotional connection. Thereafter, a child's emotions are rarely in short supply. Toddler tantrums over the baked beans on their plate so much as touching the fish fingers, or being given the wrong coloured beaker for breakfast, can leave parents feeling sorely tempted to lie down on the floor and have a tantrum themselves. For the toddler, the strength of their emotions can feel overwhelming; they have no idea how to manage them.

As children get older, their emotions become more complex, and teenagers often experience extremely powerful feelings, including incredible highs followed by crashing lows. Having a teenager in the house may feel like living in the foothills of a smouldering Mount Etna. Behind the scenes there's a lot happening developmentally

---

49 'Fighting anxiety: Children's Mental Health Week', *Youth and Children's Work*, February 2020, youthandchildrens.work.

with many parts of the brain being remodelled and rewired to work in the more complex way needed for adult life.

Nicola Morgan, author of *Blame My Brain*, describes this process as being akin to a tree suddenly growing and branching out in the spring.[50] There is huge growth at the start of puberty; in fact, too many connections are made which then have to be cut back. The cells the brain doesn't need or doesn't use, gradually fall away. As the experts in *Gardeners' World* will tell you, pruning a tree will leave it with fewer branches, but those that are left will grow stronger. Scientists believe that this pruning process in the brain is even more important than the growth itself.

In late adolescence, the nerve cells left in the brain after pruning thicken and are coated with a fatty substance called myelin to make them strong – a bit like insulation on an electric wire. This process, called myelination, is important because it helps nerve cells to transmit information faster and enables more complex brain processes. What makes this uncomfortable (for both parents and teenagers) is the uneven way in which it happens: it starts at the back of the brain and moves gradually to the front. And the very last part of the brain to mature is the prefrontal cortex, the brain's rational centre, which is responsible for decision making, self-control and mood-modulation.[51]

Because their pre-frontal cortex develops later, studies have shown that teenagers use another part of their brain instead – the amygdala. The amygdala is sometimes called the 'alarm bell' of the brain and it is responsible for our gut reactions and raw emotion. So rather than using their prefrontal cortex – the brain's rational centre – our teenagers will, most of the time, think with their feelings.

This late development of the pre-frontal cortex also affects how teenagers handle social situations, because they miss early

50 Nicola Morgan, *Blame My Brain: The Amazing Teenage Brain Revealed* (Walker Books, 2013), pp28–29.
51 Alexandra Sifferlin, 'Why Teenage Brains Are So Hard to Understand', *Time Magazine*, 8 September 2017.

cues of emotion – for example, signs that someone is becoming upset or annoyed. An interesting experiment shows that adults and teenagers use a different part of the brain when interpreting people's feelings. Whereas adults use their fully developed rational prefrontal cortex, teenagers use the limbic system (including the amygdala) to interpret emotion.[52] So when it feels like they aren't thinking things through, it's highly likely that they may simply have read the situation differently because they are trying to interpret an emotion through this lens of impulse and instinct.[53]

Dr Middleton says that when we experience 'survival instinct' emotions of extreme anxiety or frustration, our amygdala takes over – 'hijacks' – our rational mind, so that we react purely out of instinct.[54] It's why we get that sense of 'losing it' or of no longer being able to think clearly. And because teenagers use their amygdala even more than adults, they are much more prone to this. It's as if a match is struck, and in situations where the consequences are negative, our role as parents is to help them blow the match out rather than fan it further into flame, encouraging them to take time to calm down and think things through before they do something they later regret. While they can't help their emotions, they can learn not to let them take over. Except in emergencies, emotions aren't designed to be in control; the rational mind generally does a much better job!

Research by psychologist Dr John Gottman shows a strong link between how we manage our emotions and our happiness in life.[55] When children learn to have more control over their emotions, they have a buffer against life's knocks and are more confident and self-

52 Kathryn Scherf, Joshua Smyth and Mauricio Delgado, 'The Amygdala: An Agent of Change in Adolescent Neural Networks', *Hormones and Behaviour*, June 2013.
53 Deborah Yurgelun-Todd, 'Emotional and cognitive changes during adolescence', *Current Opinion in Neurobiology*, vol.17, no.2, May 2007, pp251–257.
54 Kate Middleton, speaking at New Wine Regional Leadership Conference, 12 March 2019, London.
55 Susan Chira, 'Parent & Child Study Finds Benefits In Emotional Control', *New York Times*, 26 May 1994.

'That's easy for you to say, with your fully developed rational prefrontal cortex!'

assured. As parents, we have a key role in helping our children learn to manage and regulate their feelings (and during the pandemic with emotions – both ours and our children's – running high, knowing how to handle this with our children has been even more of a pressing issue than usual). So where do we start? Rather than panicking and enrolling for a crash course in child psychology, Gottman suggests some simple dos and don'ts.[56]

Do recognize negative emotions as an opportunity to connect

When one of my children was feeling sad or worried, my desire to keep the show on the road meant I would often minimize the problem or try to distract them in the hope they would forget it. Thankfully, my children are brighter than me and this tactic rarely worked.

It has been said that unexpressed emotions do not die, they are simply buried and come out later in uglier ways, and if we try to prevent our children experiencing a difficult emotion, rather than going away, it will pop up again, often unexpectedly and at the worst of times. For parents, it is so much better to bring our child's issue out into the open and use it as an opportunity to deepen our relationship with them.

Dan looked back on the early years of parenting his two children Jayden and Zane.

'Jayden was such an easy child. We saw our friends struggling with their children's tantrums and honestly felt a bit smug. Then Zane was born. Life with him was so different. He'd hurl himself on the floor, kicking and screaming, at even the simplest request. We eventually decided enough was enough and made a plan. Whenever he kicked off, we sent him to his bedroom and didn't allow him back in the room until he'd calmed down. While this met our need for peace and quiet, I now realize that it wasn't the best tactic. It didn't stop him being

56 April Eldemir, '3 Dos and Don'ts for Raising Emotionally Intelligent Kids', *The Gottman Institute,* 10 October 2016.

upset, but more than that, it gave him the message that he was on his own with feelings he didn't know how to control. Trying to stay calm and connect with him would have been a much better strategy.'

When it's possible (generally not in the heat of the moment), we can take the opportunity to talk to our children about their feelings. Some will engage readily, but in my experience, this is easier said than done. Younger children may not have the vocabulary or self-awareness to explain, and even if teenagers are prepared to talk, the chances are we won't be their confidante of choice. But even if a full-blown therapy session isn't possible, we can at least try to read their body language and acknowledge their feelings.

Talking to our children about their feelings also helps avoid another issue that underlies so many emotional health issues in our culture – a *fear* of emotions, especially anxiety. When a natural healthy reaction becomes a fear trigger, we try to supress what we feel and a vicious circle of anxiety develops.

Don't punish, dismiss, or scold your child for being emotional

Sociable and with a sunny disposition, 15-year-old Jem was always a delight to have around, but when he came home that evening, it was as if another person had taken him over. He was in a mood, irritable with his siblings, and stormed upstairs to his bedroom saying that he didn't want any tea – his mum's cooking was rubbish. His parents had always set clear standards of behaviour for him, and in Greta, his mother's, mind he'd crossed a line. Charging up the stairs after him, she flung open the bedroom door and told him he was grounded for the rest of the week. Over the next few days, Jem kept to his room. It was only after a chance conversation with another parent that Greta discovered that not only had Jem's best friend gone off with his girlfriend, but Jem had been dropped from the football team on the same day. Her heart sank as she realized that telling him off when he'd obviously been so upset had only made things a whole lot worse.

Feeling frustrated with their teenager's emotional volatility and the shadow it casts over the whole household is something that many parents will identify with. Everything in us wants to tackle this head on and shake them out of it, taking away all privileges and grounding them for a decade. Gottman advises against this. While we can (and must) set limits on their behaviour, they can't choose how they *feel*. Emotions aren't bad in themselves – they are part of being human – so if we punish them, dismiss their feelings, or label their emotions as bad, we're in danger of giving them the message that they are bad as well.[57]

Do help your child label their emotions

How do you describe what it feels like to be scared, sad or excited? Feelings are abstract, and if it's hard for us, as adults, to put how we are feeling into words, it's much more so for our children, particularly little ones. Our 6-year-old may complain of a tummy ache or of being too hot one minute and too cold the next, and although it's possible that the yoghurt they'd eaten was past its sell-by date, or the thermostat on the radiator is on the blink, the more likely explanation is that they are feeling anxious. Unable to figure out what is wrong, they create a narrative to fit it, even if it's wide of the mark.

As parents, we can help our children identify their emotions, positive as well as negative, and give them a name. One mum told me that her tip for doing this with younger children is to get them to imagine what the villain or the hero in a film is feeling at a particular moment in the plot. This is a first step in helping them name those emotions for themselves. Of course, they will find certain feelings easier to identify than others. A 5-year-old's happiness at seeing her granny or sadness about dropping her ice cream on the pavement will be relatively easy for her to name, but butterflies in her tummy about a 'monster' under the bed may be less easy for her to describe.

57 April Eldemir, '3 Dos and Don'ts'.

Don't convey judgment or frustration

Maybe it should be no surprise that our children generally save their BAFTA-winning displays of emotion for the most inconvenient, and sometimes outright embarrassing, times. School pick-up time seems to be a favourite, along with unexpected encounters with our boss at the ATM or bus journeys under the disparaging gaze of every passenger who has the misfortune to be on the number nine with us that day. But even if, from our perspective, our offspring's emotional outburst seems irrational, we can try to put ourselves in their shoes and see the issue from their point of view.

When Evie first went to primary school, she worked herself into a frenzy about not knowing where to put her lunch box. Her level of anxiety seemed totally over the top as her mother explained it for the sixth time that morning: there was a special place for everyone to put their lunch box and the teacher would show her where it was. The hysterics continued and Evie's mum could feel her temper rising, but she managed to tell herself that even though it was a non-issue for her, it was obviously a huge deal for Evie. Taking her daughter into the classroom, she explained the problem to the teacher and it was quickly sorted out.

Do set limits and problem-solve

While we don't want to set limits on our children's feelings, it *is* our job to set limits on their behaviour. They can't control how they feel, but we can teach them to choose how to respond by laying down some ground rules. For example, 'You can be as mad as you want, but don't hit your sister', or 'I know you're cross that you lost the game, but it's not OK to throw the console at the TV.'

We can also encourage them to think through their responses so they can express their feelings better next time. For example, 'I know you're angry, but instead of kicking the wall, why not go and kick the football in the back yard?' Coaching them to choose their response gives them a measure of autonomy and helps them regain some control in a world that seems unfair or in which they feel powerless.

Don't underestimate your child's ability to learn and grow

One of the best ways to help children learn about and express their feelings is to model healthy emotional engagement ourselves – and during the pandemic we'll certainly have had the challenge of doing this by the bucketload! Our children have all the raw material to be able to develop into emotionally mature adults – they simply need a listening ear, a hand to hold, and a parent who can help grow that capacity in them.

One last reflection on the need to encourage our children to express their emotions concerns boys. In our family, the XY chromosome is alive and well; three of our four children are boys and I have also gained a son-in-law and a grandson, so I come from the perspective of having had a ringside view of the male journey through childhood and adolescence. Many boys and men are adept at handling their emotions and being vulnerable with friends, just as there are girls and women who find these things difficult, but generally speaking, a specific issue for parents of boys is how to encourage their development in a society that can sacrifice emotional wellbeing on the altar of 'masculinity'.

Mike has a great group of friends who meet up for a drink on a Friday night. They play darts, chat about sport, and there is a lot of lad banter. He said, 'I love my mates, they're the best guys to hang out and have fun with. But recently I split up with my girlfriend and I was shocked to realize that I didn't have anyone to talk to about it'. Of course, there will be exceptions, but there are many boys who, like Mike, have good friends to laugh and joke with but no one with whom they can be vulnerable when life is tough.

Research shows that when boys embrace a misleading message about what it means to be a man, it can affect their mental wellbeing.[58] Our boys need to see involved, emotionally confident dads or dad figures who recognize that acknowledging and sharing their feelings is as vital to their overall health as a session at the gym. They need parents who give them the vital message that sometimes big boys – and girls – *do* cry. It's OK to be emotional.

58 Jon Johnson, 'What is toxic masculinity?', *Medical News Today*, 21 June 2020, medicalnewstoday.com.

ACTION POINTS

It's OK to be Emotional

- *Label your own emotions.* Increasing the vocabulary we use when speaking to our children about our feelings helps them work out and vocalize how they themselves feel. So rather than simply saying 'I'm fine' after a stressful day, we can explain 'I've been feeling a bit irritable today because work has been very busy.'

- *Accept your child's emotional responses.* Everyone has a different temperament and if your child's is very different to your own it's important to recognize and accept their emotions – especially if they are more emotionally sensitive than you.

- *Use music as a balm.* If your family enjoys listening to music, take full advantage of this. Studies have found that listening to relaxing music results in a reduction in overall anxiety, slows the heart rate, reduces blood pressure and lowers levels of the stress hormone cortisol. Try classical music or instrumental music as well as your current favourites.

- *Deep breathing slows the heartbeat and expels stress chemicals.* With younger children, try doing 'dragon breaths' when they are stressed, taking a big breath in and an even bigger one out.

- *Acknowledge your toddler's strong emotions.* After a tantrum is over, children will recover better if you let them talk about it.

- *Anger tips for your child.* Talk with your child about what triggers their anger and discuss how they can take action to manage it. For example, you can encourage them to:
  1. count to 10
  2. walk away from the situation
  3. talk to a trusted person about it
  4. breathe slowly and deeply
  5. go to a private place to calm down

  If you see your child starting to get angry, point this out to them as this will give them the chance to try out these strategies.

ACTIVITY

Ask your child to make a 'feelings thermometer'. Many children are helped by being able to rank their emotions on a scale of 1 to 10 – 1 being happy and 10 being very sad, or 1 being peaceful and 10 being furious. With older children, you can simply use this analogy verbally. For example, if you leave your mobile phone at work and have to go back for it, announce that you're at a 6.

HEALTHY BODY, HEALTHY MIND

SLEEP

Sleep directly impacts the mental and physical development of children.[59] Studies have shown that children who get enough sleep have improved mental and physical health.[60] They can concentrate for longer, have better problem-solving abilities, are more able to make positive decisions and can develop healthy relationships with other people. Lack of sleep can cause irritability, increased stress, forgetfulness, difficulties with learning and low motivation. Extended periods of lack of sleep can also contribute to anxiety and depression.[61]

- *Establish a routine.* Irregular bedtimes are a recipe for an unhealthy sleep pattern. While allowing the occasional special late night, do your best to keep the same times for bedtime and waking up.

- *Create a restful environment.* The key three components are cool, dark and quiet. Dimming lights in the house during the evening can be a good part of the wind down routine.

- *Keep screens out of the bedroom.* A phone by the bed is bad news on two counts. First, the temptation to check TikTok in the early hours is a big sleep-distraction; second, research has shown that the blue light given off

59 Danielle Pacheco, 'Children and Sleep', *Sleep Foundation*, 24 September 2020, sleepfoundation.org.
60 Rachel Dawkins, 'The Importance of Sleep for Kids, *Johns Hopkins Medicine*, 12 March 2018, hopkinsallchildrens.org.
61 SickKids staff, 'Sleep: Benefits and recommended amounts', *About Kids Health*, 13 April 2020, aboutkidshealth.ca.

by our screens plays havoc with sleep. This light tricks our brains into thinking it's daytime by blocking the release of melatonin, the hormone that helps us relax and wind down.[62] Buy a multi-charger for all the family to charge their phones in downstairs at night. And if your child relies on their phone to wake them up in the morning, buy them an alarm clock.

- *Gradually wind-down in the evenings.* Avoid caffeine, fast and loud music, strenuous exercise, or a big meal just before bed.

- *Remember that teenagers have different sleep patterns.* Sleep is seriously important for all of us of course, but a good night's sleep is especially important for teenagers. They need eight to ten hours a night, and a lack of sleep can really affect their ability to pay attention and to study. Sleep deprivation also affects the development of the frontal lobe, which can make risky behaviour even more impulsive than normal.[63] During adolescence, their bodies naturally tend towards staying up late and sleeping longer – they're not being lazy. Establishing good sleep habits and routines is therefore even more important for teenagers, but hard for them to put into practice.

- *If you or your children have sleep problems, get some advice.* One of the most important things to know about sleep is that it's possible to train ourselves to sleep better.

---

62 'Does the Light From a Phone or Computer Make it Hard to Sleep?', *TeensHealth*, kidshealth.org.
63 Eric Suni, 'Teens and Sleep', *Sleep Foundation*, 5 August 2020, sleepfoundation.org.

'Sorry Officer, you know how it is with kids.
They need your full attention.'

CHAPTER 7

LET'S TALK

The author Michael Morpurgo tells a wonderful story about the origin of one his most famous books. A charity he is involved with gives activity breaks to children growing up in the inner city and one year, Billy, a boy from Birmingham, came to stay on the Morpurgos' farm. He was severely withdrawn and had a stutter. As Michael read a story to the children, he couldn't help noticing this little boy sitting alone at the back, sad, isolated and in his own anxious world. Michael's heart went out to him. Then one evening, as he was walking near the stables, he stopped in his tracks. In the moonlight, he saw Billy sitting on his own with a gentle mare. Michael described the scene which so moved him:

> He was talking to the horse, one to one, about what he had done on the farm that day. No stutter – words flowing out of him. I summoned his teachers and we hid in the vegetable garden to watch them ... The boy wasn't being judged or mocked. He trusted this creature. The horse wasn't understanding, but was listening. She knew she must not move away.[64]

64 Kate Kellaway, '*War Horse* author Michael Morpurgo on the hidden history behind Steven Spielberg's Oscar contender', *The Guardian*, 8 January 2012, guardian. com.

The very essence of being a parent means that we spend a lot of time talking to our children. It's a normal and necessary part of family life – we have plans to share, skills to teach and information to give them. But there are also times when we need to pause and let them do the talking. Just because their voice is small, it doesn't mean that they shouldn't be heard.

No doubt we'll all have had the experience of engaging animatedly in conversation with someone only to find their attention drifting to something more exciting behind our left shoulder. It leaves us feeling invisible and a little foolish. But I hope we've also had the reverse experience of someone looking deep into our soul as they listen to us. When that happens, it gives us an incredible sense of worth and significance. And we can do the same for our children when we listen to them.

This doesn't mean changing the family dynamics and appointing our child as interim CEO of the family – we are still the parents. The principle is to give them the opportunity to be heard – to express their feelings and ideas without them being dismissed. However wonderful, wild or weird these are, when their opinions are acknowledged it gives them dignity and self-esteem. When they are ignored, we risk damaging their sense of worth.

Listening is a skill worth perfecting because there's nothing quite like it for steadying and helping a child think through their emotions. In our fast-paced, solution-oriented, instant society this can feel counter-intuitive, so here are a few reminders to help us on the way.

1. Find a good time

Life is busy and our children rarely choose the best time to talk to us – particularly if they are upset. My children seemed to impart important information at the most inconvenient moments – on the way out to a doctor's appointment, just as visitors were about to arrive, or when I was turning onto a busy roundabout in rush-hour traffic. Jenny, mum to two teenage girls, said: 'I remember one of our girls starting a major conversation just as I was leaving for work. I realized I was unlikely to get this moment again, so decided to call work and let them know I'd be in later.' Of course, not everyone would be able to do that, but another option may have been to agree a time with her daughter later that day to revisit the conversation. And, crucially, to resolve not to postpone it under any circumstances.

2. Find a good place

We can also avoid distractions by choosing a good place for a listening conversation. Sometimes this might be somewhere familiar in the home. Rob Parsons remembers a woman telling him about an old wooden chair in her parents' kitchen. It was the chair her mother had sat in to nurse her when she was a baby. After going to school, she used to run home and sit in that chair talking to her mother as she made the evening meal. Later, as a teenager, she often sat there and poured out her heart to her parents. They called it 'the talking chair'.[65]

Theresa has twin girls, one an extrovert and one an introvert, and both were bullied at school. Megan, the extrovert, told her every detail – who'd said what to whom and how it made her feel. Lydia was a different kettle of fish. Theresa had to work hard to get a single syllable from her. While they were walking the dog together one evening, however, Lydia's guard came down at last and she began to share with her mother some of the things she'd been going through. Whether it's going for a walk with a dog, sitting in a wooden chair, or going to a different place altogether, somewhere free from distractions is a great help in beginning the conversation.

3. Focus

Sometimes the problem with listening to our children is closer to home. I remember an occasion when my daughter, Charlotte, was about 5 and she'd just returned from a friend's house where they'd

65 Rob Parsons, *The Sixty Minute Family: An Hour to Transform Your Relationships Forever* (Lion, 2010), p28.

'You can make me sit in it, but you can't force me to talk.'

seen an exciting film. It had a complicated plot involving an ice queen, an enchanted wood, a hummingbird, a knight, a castle, and a lengthy cast list besides. As we sat around the kitchen table, she began to tell us the story, unravelling the plot frame by frame and in excruciating detail. It was incredibly boring and my concentration started to wander. My eyes fell on a magazine article next to me on the table with the headline '10 Ways to Declutter Your Home'. Our home was in dire need of a Marie Kondo makeover at that point, so I read the first few lines and was immediately hooked. Charlotte continued for a while without missing a beat but then she stopped.

'Mummy, you're not listening.'
'Yes, I am darling,' I said while wondering where on earth the author stored her papers in her minimalist home.
'No, you're not, Mummy. You need to listen with your eyes.'

She was right. I had completely disengaged with the exploits of the ice queen and the hummingbird, but, more so, I had disengaged with my daughter. Listening to our children means turning off the running dialogue in our head, switching off our phone, pausing our to-do list and giving our children our full attention.

While young children need eye contact, listening to teenagers is often easier when they *don't* feel put on the spot. Teenagers prefer any time or place that reduces the intensity. So a casual conversation while you are doing something else – sitting side by side in a cafe, going for a walk, perched on a breakfast bar while you are cooking – will all do the job. Some of the best conversations I had with my children as teenagers took place either when we were in the car (with no eye contact) or inconveniently late at night. Some children will readily chat about all that's going on, but with others we may need to work a little harder. And if our conversation is a one-way street, sometimes the best we can do is to simply let them know that we'll be there for them whenever they do want to talk.

4. Listen out for how they are feeling
It's important to try to understand the feelings behind our children's words or behaviour. Amir is a compliant child, but his mum, Sadia, was recently called into school by his teacher to talk about his bad behaviour. A few days later at bedtime, she took a moment to ask him how his day had been. 'I hate school,' he said, then shut his eyes. Sadia decided not to leave it there. As she gently asked a few more questions, the story tumbled out. A few weeks earlier, Amir had got up from his chair and just as another child was about to sit on it, a classmate said, 'Don't sit on Amir's chair. You'll get a disease'. Since then, he'd been living with anger, hurt and anxiety bottled up inside. After talking with his mother and getting things off his chest, Amir left for school in a much better frame of mind and fortunately it proved to be a one-off incident. Not every problem will be so easily resolved, but listening out for how our children are feeling and prompting them to share their thoughts with us is often a catalyst that enables them to move on.

Sixteen-year-old Emily was extremely anxious about attending Sixth-Form College, and teachers telling her to pull herself together and friends who'd turned their backs hadn't helped. She said that what made a big difference to her was the fact her parents listened, saw beyond the issue to the root of the problem, and took her seriously.

5. Don't try to fix it
Even if we know the solution to our child's problem, our aim isn't to fix it, but simply to allow them to talk about it. Interrupting, being dismissive, or jumping in with instant solutions can make them feel that their own thoughts on the matter are falling on deaf ears. We may find that next time they'll vote with their feet and take their problems elsewhere – or even worse, bottle up their feelings and not speak to anyone.

6. Don't have any no-go areas
One of the greatest gifts we can give our children is allowing them to feel they can talk to us about anything – no holds barred. If we feel uncomfortable with what they are saying – perhaps if they are challenging our values – it can be hard to deal with. But it is vital we try to have an open mind, giving them a safe place to talk and the dignity of being heard. Lara remembers the evening she first plucked up courage to speak to her parents about her feelings around her sexuality. She said:

> *'I knew it was going to be a hard conversation and I'd put off having it for months, but I couldn't keep it to myself anymore. I don't think it was a surprise to my parents, but they reacted so differently. My dad didn't really listen – he just blanked it at first and then tried to persuade me that I was wrong about how I felt. He told me it was 'just a phase', that I was being influenced by my friends, and that I'd grow out of it. I knew Mum was coming from the same place in many ways, but somehow she managed to put her own feelings to one side and I felt she understood. That made such a difference. I think now I could talk to her about anything.'*

Our children may well have experiences, fears and concerns that are difficult to hear about, but as parents, a good aim is to be un-shockable. As far as possible, we need to leave the door of communication open and to let them know that whatever they are struggling with, we are there to listen.

ACTION POINTS

Let's Talk

- *Use play to talk with younger children.* Spending time with and watching children as they play can throw light on how they are feeling, because they use play, as well as words, to express themselves. Children who are upset often play fighting or aggressive games with their toys. Help them open up about their worries by saying something like 'That seems very frightening' or 'That toy is acting like he is really angry.'

- *Don't take things too personally – especially with teenagers.* It's important to lower your defences, even if you feel under attack.

- *Be prepared to apologize.* If you've made a mistake or misunderstood a situation with your children, explain and say sorry. You are also role modelling what to do when they are in the wrong.

- *Concentrate on them and don't interrupt.* Stop everything else you are doing, put your phone away, make eye contact with your child, and with small children, kneel to their level. Let them finish what they are saying at their own pace.

- *Remember the acronym PLUC – Pause, Listen, Understand and Comment – when talking to teenagers.* (PLUC as it takes pluck to do this well.)

  Pause – don't just react

  Listen – to what they are saying

  Understand – ask questions to check with your child that you've understood them correctly.

  Comment – share what you think but only after you've done all the above and only if you have permission.

ACTIVITY

When all you get is a grunt in response to 'How was your day?' it may be worth asking a random question to get the conversation going. Try these:

- 'What would do you if you only had 24 hours left on earth?'
- 'What's your favourite app at the moment?'
- 'What one item would you take with you if the house was burning down?'
- 'If you could have dinner with anyone, who would you choose?'

ZIP IT

'It's all in your head.
Don't worry about it!'

'Don't be upset Mum, this is a great opportunity
for a new microwave!'

CHAPTER 8

YOU CAN'T DO IT ... YET

James had spent a happy hour in the Lego store. His grandparents had taken him into town to spend his birthday money and after much deliberation he'd settled on a Lunar Space Station. It was slightly more difficult and had far more pieces than he was used to, but as he told his grandfather, he was really good at Lego – everyone said so – and he was confident he could make it easily.

Two hours later, most of the pieces had been swept off the table in temper and lay scattered across the kitchen floor. James was now angrily kicking the empty box against the wall. The Lunar Space Station had been more difficult to assemble than he'd thought. Angry and upset he had declared it 'stupid' and refusing all offers of help, he had simply given up.

Research by psychologist Carol Dweck has shown that how our children approach learning has a direct impact on what they are able to achieve – and can therefore affect their confidence and mental wellbeing. She suggests they can adopt one of two mindsets that will either prevent them from fulfilling their potential or propel them into learning and growth.[66]

Children with a *fixed mindset* believe that our ability is predetermined – that everyone is born with a fixed amount of talent that cannot be changed. So if you are rubbish at something, nothing you do will change that. On the other hand, if you are good at something, success is guaranteed. They view every challenge as an opportunity to show off their strengths; effort is simply for those who haven't got native talent.

On the other side of the coin, children with a *growth mindset* believe that the secret of their success isn't that they are talented or clever but a result of their effort and perseverance. Skills can be learnt, and the hand they have been dealt is just the springboard for endless possibilities of growth.

The differences between a fixed mindset and a growth mindset come to the fore when children are presented with a challenge. Those with a fixed mindset tend to avoid risk and challenge because when they find a task difficult it means they aren't as clever as they thought. The task is a defining judgment of their potential; their failure means they are stupid and they blame themselves or others.

In contrast, children with a growth mindset see challenge as an opportunity to learn and difficulty as an inevitable part of the learning process. Failure means they need to try again and they persist despite, or even because of, setbacks. Apportioning blame isn't an issue and they seek help from others.

As parents, we have the opportunity to build emotional resilience in our children by helping them cultivate a growth mindset that will set them up for lifelong learning. Of course, different children may have different abilities, but it is what they believe about their ability that is crucial.

The good news is that we can do this simply by adjusting the way we praise our children and by changing the way we talk to

66 Carol Dweck, 'What Having a Growth Mindset Actually Means', *Harvard Business Review*, January 2016, leadlocal.global.

them about their achievements and struggles. Carol Dweck's study on the impact of praise found that when children were praised for their ability and cleverness they did less well in subsequent more challenging tasks than those who had been praised for their effort.[67] They were also less likely to volunteer for harder challenges. So rather than applauding a child's ability or talent, we need to focus our praise on their approach to the process of learning – their effort, perseverance and improvement. This is a far better way of helping our children fulfil their potential.

The after-school club had arranged a special session on circus skills, and the children sat spellbound as Ricki gave a breathtaking demonstration of his juggling act. Red, blue and green balls spun through the air in a beautiful dance, at times suspended as if by magic. Starting with one, then two, and for those who were good enough, three balls, he showed the children the secrets of his art. Nine-year-old Lauren found to her surprise that this skill came to her quite easily, and she couldn't wait for her dad to come home from work so she could show him what she could do.

That evening as Lauren demonstrates her newfound skill, her father will naturally want to cheer her on. Like many of us, the instinctive temptation will be to praise her talent: 'Lauren, you're brilliant at juggling!', 'You've got such a great eye for a ball!', 'That's so clever!'

Lauren will feel affirmed of course, but receiving that particular kind of praise gives her the message that it is being good at something that counts. If her father wants to praise her in a way that encourages a growth mindset, he will focus on her effort: 'Lauren, well done! You must have worked so hard to be able to do that. Juggling is really difficult and needs lots of practice. I'm so proud of you.'

Carol Dweck warns that praising children's intelligence or inherent ability is ultimately harmful to their performance as it

67 Carol Dweck, 'The Perils and Promises of Praise', *Educational Leadership*, vol.65, no.2, October 2007, pp34–39.

demotivates them. They end up not wanting to try anything difficult or take risks for fear of looking stupid. She comments:

> If parents want to give their children a gift, the best thing they can do is to teach their children to love challenges, be intrigued by mistakes, enjoy effort, and keep on learning. That way, their children don't have to be slaves of praise. They will have a lifelong way to build and repair their own confidence.[68]

While there were many things my husband, Richard, and I got wrong as parents, one thing I hope we got right was seeking to praise our children's efforts in all areas of life. As well as celebrating sports wins, performances at school plays and academic achievements, we'd often try to include a high five simply for their perseverance, hard work or attempting something new. So, when exams came along, we made the point by having a pizza out or some other kind of celebration *before* results day.

The danger when we praise a child's talents rather than their efforts is that we end up giving them a label. They grow up with the fixed mindset that they are good at maths, hopeless at languages, not musical, etc. Labels like these can end up defining them and putting a glass ceiling on their growth and learning.

Even the most accomplished and successful people understand that hard work and effort is necessary in order to succeed. Spanish musician Pablo de Sarasate, who began playing the violin at the age of five and attended the famous Paris Conservatoire aged 12, commented, 'For 37 years I've practised 14 hours a day and now they call me a genius.'[69] Mozart also dedicated thousands of hours to practice. 'People make a great mistake who think that my art has come easily to me,' he once wrote to his father. 'Nobody has devoted

---

68 Carol Dweck, *The Mindset: The new psychology of success* (Ballantine, 2006), pp179–180.
69 Manfredi Ricca and Rebecca Robins, *Meta-Luxury: Brands and the Culture of Excellence* (Palgrave, 2012), p72.

so much time and thought to composition as I.'[70] Speaking on a TV chat show two centuries later, singer and songwriter Ed Sheeran seemed to agree: 'When people say that artists are born with talent – you're not! You have to really learn and really practise.'[71]

If we give our children what is known as 'process praise', we'll focus on the tactics they used. So, if they've done well in maths homework, we might ask questions such as 'What method did you use?', 'Did you have to change your approach?', or 'What questions did you find hard?' On the other hand, if they are struggling with a piece of homework, giving them process praise might be along the lines of 'Well done for trying. I know you haven't managed to work it out yet – try an easier question first and then have another go.'

Process praise reminds them that life is a journey where they learn along the way, and we don't expect them to nail things first time. If they don't succeed, it is no reflection on them as a person. The truth is that having brains and talent are just the beginning. It is when we struggle to learn new skills that new neural connections are made in the brain which enable continued learning and growth.[72] And as well as learning new skills, this is about building confidence. Once one building block is in place, other blocks can then be built on top. So, the more we give our children opportunities to see what they can do, the more their confidence grows.

When our children find something challenging, the phrase 'I can't do it' becomes all too familiar. As parents, one of the greatest ways of building emotional resilience and wellbeing in them, not just for today but for all the challenges ahead, is to add one little word that changes everything: 'You can't do it ... yet.'

70 Gordon Stobart, *The Expert Learner* (Expanding Educational Horizons) (Open University Press, 2014), p29.
71 'Series 3 Episode 09', *The Jonathan Ross Show*, ITV, 13 October 2012.
72 Mengia-S Rioult-Pedotti et al., 'Strengthening of horizontal cortical connections following skills learning', *Nature Neuroscience*, vol.1, July 1998, pp230–234, nature.com.

ACTION POINTS

You Can't Do It ... Yet

- *Remember that important word* 'yet'. Reassure your child that not being able to do something now, doesn't mean they'll never be able to do it or that they're a failure. 'You don't know how to do it ... yet' communicates possibility and the sense that the only thing standing between them and the thing they want to do is time and practice.

- *Explain the brain science.* Children will often be afraid of failure, so explaining that mistakes will actually help their brains grow and enable them to learn better will do much to reassure them and get them feeling excited about learning and practising new things.

- *Remind them of past successes.* Children can very quickly become discouraged about their ability to do new things, so take time to give them clear examples of where their hard work and patience led to success. For example, 'When you started pre-school you couldn't write your name, but look at how you can write it now!' or 'Maths may be hard work, but remember how much you helped your uncle calculate how much wood he needed to repair the garage door.'

- *Help them see mistakes as opportunities.* Talk about setbacks or difficulties in a matter-of-fact way without catastrophizing. Encourage your children to think about what they can do to make a difference next time or avoid the difficulty.

ACTIVITY

1. Ask your child to write down a number of things they can't do or can't do properly. (For pre-schoolers, ask them to tell you what these are and write it down for them.)

2. Now make a colourful chart on a large piece of paper, listing each thing. At the end of each item, leave a blank space.

3. Draw and cut out several colourful or glittery squares of the word *yet*.

4. Give your child the pieces and have an 'I can't do it ... yet' ceremony with your child sticking the word *yet* into the blank space.

'Sorry Sir, it's just my mum telling me I'm amazing.'

CHAPTER 9

THE POWER OF PRAISE

An ancient proverb says that our words have the power of life and death,[73] and almost 3,000 years after it was written experts agree that the words spoken to us significantly impact our mental wellbeing. Harsh, critical and negative words cause the stress hormone cortisol to be released in our brains, whereas kind, positive and affirming words have the opposite effect, bringing us life and wellbeing.[74]

Every day our children will hear things said to or about them – by parents, siblings, teachers, youth leaders, sports coaches, strangers and, of course, their friends. And whether it's done face-to-face, via a 6'x3' illuminated screen, or in other ways, each of these messages impact their emotional wellbeing in one way or another – for good or ill.

Emma climbed into bed with a sick feeling in her stomach. She knew it would have been better to leave her phone downstairs, but somehow, she couldn't bring herself to do that. Instead, she plugged it in, laid it beside her pillow, closed her eyes and waited. As the

73 Proverbs 18:21, *The Holy Bible*, New International Version Anglicized (Biblica, 2011).
74 Therese J. Borchard, 'Words Can Change Your Brain', *Psych Central*, 27 May 2019, psychcentral.com.

minutes ticked by, she dug her nails into her arm. And then it came … the familiar beep that was impossible to ignore. Slowly, she lifted the phone. The words that had started on the group chat as an unkind joke seemed now to have taken on a life of their own, and they hurt.

I would hazard a guess that as adults, most of us can remember all too easily unkind things that have been said to us. It certainly gives the lie to the saying that children have been subjected to over the years: 'Sticks and stones may break my bones, but words will never hurt me.' But while, when I was young, the taunts of the school bully were mostly confined to the playground, the phone in their pocket means that for children today, a bully can follow them home and through the front door. On the bus, during supper, whilst doing their homework, in bed – there is no escape. Online bullying takes place on social media sites, games and messaging apps, and it affects children of both primary and secondary school age 24/7.[75]

The stress of living in a constant state of fear or upset can have a profound effect on a victim's mental wellbeing. In one survey, 60% of bullied children said that it affected their mental health[76] and research has shown that it can lead to a sobering list of issues including lack of confidence and self-esteem, loss of appetite, poor sleep, anxiety and depression.[77] If we know or suspect that our child is being bullied, it is therefore vital for their wellbeing that we take action to support them. (See appendix for information about organizations giving help and support with regard to bullying.)

It's not hard to see why bullying is so damaging. First, our children are a work in progress, their sense of self is fragile and evolving, and

75 Emma J. Scott and Jeremy Dale, 'Childhood bulling: implications for general practice', *British Journal of General Practice*, vol.66, no.651, 2016, pp504–505.
76 'The Annual Bullying Survey 2018', *Ditch the Label*, June 2018, ditchthelabel. org. .
77 D. Wolke et al., 'Bullying in elementary school and psychotic experiences at 18 years: a longitudinal, population-based cohort study', *Psychol Med.*, vol.44, no.10, July 2014, pp2199–2211.

they are not yet secure in their identity, so unkind words can leave deep scars.[78] Second, children generally take their experiences of the world at face value and are much more likely than adults to accept a bully's words or actions as gospel truth. And finally, children spend thousands of hours in the company of friends whose approval is hugely significant to them. It goes without saying, then, that their friends' disapproval is deeply damaging.[79]

We have the opportunity every day to use our words to impact our children's self-esteem – but it's not always easy! When we're late for school, the children are squabbling, our teenager is still in bed, and we can't find the car keys, even the most saintly, serene parent would find it almost impossible not to slip into the groove of nagging and criticism. Looking back at when my children were little, I need to put my hand up to say 'guilty as charged'. But while there will be mornings when we lose our rag and say things we regret, the trick is not to allow this to become the norm. If we are always on our children's backs and pointing out what they're doing wrong, it does nothing to build their sense of self-worth and, ironically, is less likely to spur them into action. Giving positive rather than negative input is not about failing to put boundaries in place, overlooking deliberate misdemeanours, or giving our children unmerited or insincere praise, but looking out for ways we can encourage and affirm them.

When I spoke to 18-year-old Chloe about her journey with anorexia, she said there were many contributing factors, but reflected in particular about the issue of family dynamics and her relationship with her father. She said:

'My parents were products of their own childhoods, distant and never expressing much love. Looking back, I'd have loved my dad to have

78 G. Salmon et al., 'Bullying in schools: self-reported anxiety, depression, and self-esteem in secondary school children', *BMJ*, 317, 3 October 1998.
79 Calli Tzani-Peplasi, 'Childhood bullying can cause lifelong psychological damage: How to spot the signs and move on', *News GP*, 21 August 2018, racgp.org.

been more generous with his words to me. He'd congratulate me when I did well at school and got another A or A*, or when I won a swimming race, but never any more than that. I never felt affirmed as a person. That would have been so good.'

As parents, we have a wonderful opportunity to build our children's emotional resilience simply through what we say to them. Positive affirmation can act as a buffer not only against the school bully but against all kinds of knocks in life. Researchers say that we each need at least five positive things said to us to counteract one negative comment.[80] The world is doing a pretty good job already at making it hard to keep a healthy ratio, so as parents we need to step in and rectify the balance.

In saying kind, encouraging and affirming things to our children, we make rich deposits in their emotional lives. When it feels like the world is against them, our words can remind them that they are valued and that at least one person sees the good in them and has their back.

If we have more than one child, they can be chalk and cheese, and if one is compliant we may find it easier to affirm them than we do their testing sibling. But that testing child needs our encouragement and praise just as much, and it's vital we give it to them. So often, all the testing child hears are negative comments – 'Don't hit your sister!', 'Don't kick a ball in the house!' It may take a degree of determination and energy on our part, but even if it means digging deep beneath the crisp packets, coke cans, wet towels and smelly trainers in our teenager's bedrooms to find something to be positive about – their enthusiasm, liveliness, kindness, loyalty to their friends – the impact on their wellbeing can be powerful.

A couple of years ago, I witnessed an incredible example of the potential of words to bring about a change in a child's self-esteem.

80 Rachel Wise, 'Evidence-Based Approach Improves Student Behavior and Engagement', *Education and Behaviour*, 15 June 2017, educationandbehaviour.com.

'*Great tantrum, Sarah!*'

I'd been speaking on this subject to a group of parents and a young mum came up to me in the break and started to cry. She told me that she had two girls; the older one was a delight, but the youngest was driving her crazy:

> 'She argues with her sister, her bedroom is a mess, she's rude and inconsiderate, and she's always in trouble at school. In fact, her behaviour is causing conflict between me and my husband. We're so exasperated with her that for the last year instead of calling her by her name, 'Grace', we call her 'Disgrace'. I know it's wrong, and I'm going to go home tonight and try to do things differently.'

A year later at the same annual event, as I walked through the bookshop I saw a familiar face coming towards me. She was beaming and she held the hand of a beautiful little girl with curly blonde hair who, like her mum, was grinning from ear to ear. Before I could greet them, the mum started to speak:

> 'I'm so glad to have met you again. After your talk last year, my husband and I agreed to change the way we spoke to our daughter. Even when she was behaving badly, we didn't call her 'Disgrace' but gave her real name – 'Grace'. That one decision kick-started a number of other changes and our home is now a different place. Thank you!'

Of course, the change didn't happen overnight, but that decision to speak positively to their daughter was a catalyst for a new beginning. How we speak to each other in the home matters; our words are powerful.

While the family is the primary place for our children to receive words of affirmation, the words of other people also make a difference. I recently met Lisa, who told me a wonderful story. She was a cookery teacher, had a new job in a school, and pretty soon the first parents' evening had come around. Claire's mum had booked in for one of the first appointments and Lisa was able to tell her how well her daughter was doing: 'Claire is a delight to teach. She always listens to instructions and has real talent.' The mum looked pleased, although a bit surprised, and moved on to the next desk to see the maths teacher.

Two hours later, another mum came for her appointment. 'Can you just remind me, of your daughter's name?' Lisa asked.

'Claire,' the mum replied. In that moment, Lisa realized she'd made a terrible mistake. It was *this* Claire who had been doing so well; the other Claire was different story.

> *'I realized I'd got it wrong,' Lisa said, 'but the first mother must have gone home and said something to her daughter because a fascinating thing began to happen. Claire no.1 began to change. She came to the lesson on time, with the right ingredients, and she listened and worked hard.'*

Sometime later, her mum told Lisa: 'I will never forget that parents' evening. You were the first person to say anything positive about Claire. We noticed over the following days and weeks that she started to try harder – and not just to get better marks in cookery but in all the other subjects as well.'

Experts agree that positive words can change our thinking and our behaviour. The touching end to this story is that Claire went on to become a cookery teacher herself. The sheer power of positive words not only enabled that little girl to believe in herself but allowed her to believe that change was possible.

It is important for our children's wellbeing that they learn to create a positive belief in themselves from within. In childhood, we learn behaviours that will stay with us throughout our lives, and negative beliefs about ourselves are hard to shift as we get older. In other words, what we think about ourselves is who we become. If we believe we are loved and lovable, we will behave like we are loved and lovable, and we will be much better able to cope when people criticise us or bring us down.

A newspaper article about the actress Dawn French included this lovely description of the power of words in her upbringing:

> When Dawn ... was fourteen years old, overweight and about to go to her first disco, her late father sat her down for a talk. She was expecting the usual father/daughter stuff about boys with high testosterone levels and what time she should be home.
>
> He did spell out what he would do to any overenthusiastic lad who dared lay a finger on the young Dawn. But it was what he said next that had such a lasting effect on her life.
>
> He told her she was uncommonly beautiful, the most precious thing in his life, that he prized her above everything and was proud to be her father.
>
> No father could have given his daughter a more valuable start in life. Instead of approaching adolescence as the short, fat girl, who couldn't get a boyfriend, Dawn was secure in the knowledge that she was loved for who she was, not for what she looked like.
>
> That confidence has remained throughout her adult life. And, yes, she is uncommonly beautiful. It is a soft, warm beauty, enhanced by a ready, generous smile.
>
> 'How wise of my father to say that,' she reflects. 'It affected my whole life. How could you not come out of it well-equipped to deal with life, when you felt so loved and supported?'[81]

81 Lester Middlehurst, 'Interview with Dawn French', *Daily Mail Weekend*, 4 May 1996, pp6–7, mailonline.newspaperdirect.com.

ACTION POINTS

The Power of Praise

- *Send your children texts or written notes of encouragement.* The advantage of an encouraging text sent to a grumpy 16-year-old is that they can go back to it when they're in a better frame of mind. And a note in your daughter's rucksack or a message on a banana in your son's lunchbox may just help them through a difficult afternoon at school.

- *Look for something positive to praise or encourage.* On days of stomping tantrums or teenage strops it can be hard to find positive things to say your children, but finding something to praise them for can improve their sense of wellbeing. It can be about the simplest or more important things:

  * 'Well done! You did a great job laying the table.'
  * 'I noticed you sharing your chocolate – you're very generous.'
  * 'I loved the way you looked out for Dan and passed the ball to him. You're a great team player.'
  * 'I know you didn't want to leave the party early, but thank you for being trustworthy and getting home on time.'
  * 'You are beautiful – inside and out.'

- *Stay calm*. Speaking calmly to your children (which, if we're honest, isn't the easiest thing to do when their mission in life seems to be to drive us mad) does much to avoid turning our home into a constant battleground. Children who live in a hostile environment are more likely to feel anxious and insecure.

- *Recognize the power of touch in communicating reassurance, comfort and empathy*. Touch is known to reduce stress, and while our words are important, don't forget that a simple hug communicates safety and security. When our children are little, it's easy to find moments to give them a hug as we wash a grazed knee, snuggle up on the sofa together, or play rough and tumble games, but as they get older it can become more difficult. There may be a few eye-rolls, but most teenagers really need the occasional wisely-timed hug. As one 13-year-old boy said: 'My parents don't hug me anymore as they think I'm too old, but when no one's looking I wish they still would'.

- *Non-verbal praise works too*. Give them a high five, a pat on the shoulder or do a celebratory dance.

ACTIVITY

Make your child a treasure box. Store special birthday cards that they have received and encouraging letters or messages from school, church, friends or family. Pass this on to them when they are older and encourage them to keep adding to it for themselves. Encourage teenagers to find a way of doing the same.

ZIP IT

'You're too young to know what you're talking about.'

'I kind of wish I hadn't thrown the TV out as a punishment.'

CHAPTER 10

THAT'S THE LINE

It was their first family holiday abroad and excitement had been mounting for weeks. After a long, hot journey, they finally arrived at their hotel. The girls were desperate to explore, so leaving the unpacking for later, Matt grabbed the swimming stuff and he and Kate headed off to the pool with them. The sight that greeted their eyes was a far cry from the blue oasis of peace and calm that the website had led them to expect. Red-striped hotel towels staked a claim to every available sun lounger, and the pool teemed with shrieking children in neon swimsuits – admittedly, having the time of their lives. After a stressful few minutes, Kate eventually spotted a shady patch of grass where they could set up base.

Sitting the girls down, she and Matt began to lay down the ground rules. While Annie and Lauren could swim, neither could manage more than a width. And their youngest, Jade, still needed buoyancy aids to keep her afloat. Looking them in the eye, Matt put on his stern headteacher voice and carefully showed them a line of bricks dividing the grassy play area from the stone edge of the pool.

'Girls, you can go this far and no further. You can play on the grass, you can play in the sand pit, and you can play on the swings. But no one is to cross this line without me or Mummy with them. If you do, there will be no swimming for the rest of the day. Is that clear?'

Three little heads nodded in solemn agreement.

What happened next is probably, in different contexts, all too familiar to most parents. Jade stood up, gave her father a long hard stare, raised a chubby little leg to take one foot off the grass … and stepped over the line onto the edge of the pool.

It was an act of defiance that said so much, holding both a challenge and an underlying question:

'I know where the line is that I must not cross. You have made it very clear to me. But I need to know that you really mean it. Your job as parents is to put boundaries in place and make sure we stick to them. But I am a kid and it's my job to test those boundaries'.

This was almost a sacred moment. Jade was waiting for a reaction from her parents, and it was vital that she was not disappointed. The last thing Kate and Matt wanted to do was to follow through and call an end to swimming for the afternoon on day one of the holiday. At the time, it certainly didn't put them in the running for Mummy and Daddy of the Year Award. But they knew there was potentially more at stake. How we set and maintain boundaries with our children has a direct impact on their development and wellbeing.

Experts tell us that there are three basic styles of parenting.[82] Our own style will be influenced by our upbringing as well as by our temperament and personality.

At one end of the spectrum is the *authoritarian* parent. This parent is the sergeant major of the family, often a perfectionist who likes to be in control. There are rules for everything: shoes arranged in size order in the hall; coats hung on named pegs; the rabbit cleaned out

---

82 Diane Baumrind, 'Current patterns of parental authority', *Developmental Psychology*, vol.4, 1971, pp1–103.

on Wednesdays; and bedrooms to be tidied on Saturdays. Each rule is enforced rigidly, with strict punishments for anyone marching boldly – or sneaking quietly – across the line. In this home, parents will use phrases like 'Because I said so' or 'Don't ask why. Just do it'. The advantage of this style of parenting is that the rules are clear, and everyone knows what is expected of them. But it comes at a price. The children can feel hemmed in and suffocated, having no freedom for individuality, creativity or independent thought. The pressure of living up to the rules and expectations of authoritarian parent can impact their emotional wellbeing, with higher levels of depression and anxiety being experienced later in life.[83]

At the other end of the spectrum is the *permissive* style of parenting. Children with permissive parents may well be the envy of their peers. Their mums and dads are relaxed and *laissez-faire*, there are very few rules, and even then, few consequences for breaking them. At the extreme, this kind of parenting can masquerade as indifference. Whilst the children have plenty of opportunity to forge independence, what they don't have is security. And nothing is more destined to breed anxiety and insecurity in our children than for there to be no boundaries. Or, if there are boundaries, for them to believe that no one cares if they cross them.

Colin, whose daughter has severe mood swings, commented:

> *'When Beth was growing up, we found we were continually treading on eggshells around her. I think we were frightened to put our foot down or even draw a line because we knew she would explode. Ironically, she tells us now that if we had done so, it would have helped her enormously.'*

We are our children's parents, not their best friends, and we make a mistake if we use their short-term happiness as a barometer of

83 Eric R. Maisel, 'Authoritarian Parent, Childhood (and Adult) Depression', *Psychology Today*, 19 February 2018, psychologytoday.com.

our own self-worth.[84] This will almost certainly mean that we sometimes take a hit in the popularity stakes. But when we do this about the things we believe are important, we will be laying a strong emotional foundation in their lives to benefit them in years to come.

The third style of parenting, and the one that has the best outcome for our children's wellbeing, is *assertive*. Assertive parents know that boundaries are important for a child's safety and sense of security, but they are set in the context of relationship. One expert said that 'rules without relationship lead to rebellion' and assertive parents know that relationship is key. They take their children's opinions into account and validate their feelings, but it is nevertheless clear that they, the parents, are in charge. They will choose their battles, setting as few rules as possible. As one dad said: 'We decided what our family values were – the things that *really* mattered to us. And then we held firm about boundaries being crossed with those things, but said yes, whenever we could, to everything else.'

The parenting principle 'Say what you mean and mean what you say' set in the context of a warm, loving, family relationship is foundational to our children's sense of security and emotional wellbeing. As parents, none of us will get this right 100% of the time. I made a number of draconian threats over the years in the heat of the moment that were impossible to follow through, and on other occasions I neglected to draw the line in the first place. But having boundaries and consequences for crossing them are vital for our children's emotional wellbeing both in the short and long term. Those boundaries are important – not just for holidays in the sun, but for life.

---

84 Patricia K. Kerig, 'Revisiting the Construct of Boundary Dissolution', *Journal of Emotional Abuse* 5:2–3, 2005, pp5–42.

ACTION POINTS

That's the Line

- *Choose your golden rules.* It's better to have a few 100% non-negotiable boundaries than lots of complicated small rules. This is much easier to enforce and means that children take the few strict boundaries seriously.

- *Take time to decide on the best consequence.* We can often feel under pressure to give an immediate response to bad behaviour, but the danger is that we end up coming out with something that isn't enforceable – 'No screens for the rest of the year!' Our children feel far more secure when they know that we don't make rash proclamations.

- *Link the consequence to the misdemeanour.* For example, 'Not helping tidy up means Mummy has to do it, so she can't play a board game with you now,' or using a phone at the meal table when it's against the family rules means the phone is surrendered for an agreed amount of time.

- *Be consistent and mean what you say.* It's important to follow through on what you say – a child soon cottons on that you won't really stop their pocket money when they misbehave if you subsequently give it to them anyway. More importantly, erratic or unpredictable reactions from their parents can lead to anxiety and insecurity.

- *Back up the other parent.* Make sure that your partner or your child's other carers respect and follow your boundaries for your children. Children can be very adept at spotting a chink in the armour and playing off one parent against the other.

- *Take a second look.* Look out for signs that your child's behaviour has a pattern to it and consider what may be causing it. For example, quarrels with siblings may be due to jealousy. And uncharacteristic rebellion from a teenager may mean that they are struggling.

- *Say the word* 'no' *sparingly.* Say *yes* to as much as possible and *no* to the things that really matter. Of course, there are times when saying *no* is completely necessary, but bear in mind that when we hear this word, our brains release stress-producing hormones, so be careful not to overuse it.

- *Remember that our children need you to be their parent, not their best friend.* This will sometimes mean that, for a time, you become their Public Enemy No.1 when it comes to rules and consequences.

ACTIVITY

Get together as a family and agree on three or four family boundaries with consequences if they are overstepped. You could make it a fun time with drinks and favourite snacks. When you involve your children in making the rules, it helps them understand why those rules are needed, and they'll be more likely to keep them. With older children and teenagers, being a part of the process has a positive impact on their self-esteem and gives them a chance to take responsibility for their own behaviour.

'I think we're ready to make this an official clique.'

CHAPTER 11

BEST FRIENDS FOREVER

Dylan's family had recently moved to the area, which meant that he started his new school halfway through the term. Year Four's buddy system meant that he was given a ready-made friend in 8-year-old Connor. Both boys were keen on football and Dylan soon discovered he had landed the jackpot; in Connor he had the class hero for a friend. The boys got on famously and Dylan was quickly accepted into the cool friendship groups. It was Connor who decided who was 'in' and who was 'out'. He was the leader of the pack; whatever playground game he suggested, everyone else would follow suit. A few weeks into term, some of the boys were kicking a ball around at the end of the school day. Connor had the ball and was making his way to the makeshift goals marked out by school sweatshirts. Dylan saw his opportunity and skilfully took possession of the ball and headed off in the opposite direction. Connor's pride was hurt. Calling foul, he lay on the floor holding his ankle and shouting abuse at Dylan for what he decided was a dangerous tackle. In that moment, Dylan went from 'in' to 'out'. He was ostracized from the group, excluded from playground games, and struggled to find other friends within the class.

Millie and Becca have been friends since they were toddlers. Their mums used to say they were joined at the hip. They were in the same class at school, had sleepovers at each other's houses at weekends, and spent most of the holidays in each other's company. As they entered the teenage years their friendship became more intense, and as a mark of their loyalty to each other they wore matching bracelets and inscribed #BFF motifs on their school bags. Neither of them noticed to begin with, but gradually, as they moved through the school years, their individual tastes and interests began to change. Millie hit puberty sooner than Becca; she became more sophisticated and was keen to expand her friendship group and extend her horizons, whereas Becca was content for life to stay as it had always been. Things came to a head at Millie's birthday party. Millie was sparkling in a new outfit, standing in the middle of the kitchen, drink in hand, surrounded by her new group of friends. Becca sat on the edge looking on; she felt an outsider and completely invisible.

Changes and challenges in friendships are a normal part of growing up. Cliques, gossip, social media sniping, expectations of who-can-say-what-to-whom and even unwritten seating arrangements on the school bus, all form part of the unfolding drama of friendship during childhood and adolescence.

As parents, it can be painful to see our children struggling with their friendships. If they don't get included or don't have anyone to hang out with it can be hard not to worry. Marina, mum to 15-year-old Freya, comments:

'Freya has a passion for justice and a heightened sense of fairness which can complicate her friendships. At school she often runs to the aid of anyone who is lonely or in trouble, even dropping her existing friends in the process. While, of course, I am proud of her kindness, the knock-on effect is that most of her friends end up feeling hurt and offended. She then feels indignant and misunderstood. It's so hard seeing her struggle, and I worry that she doesn't understand what it takes to build long-lasting friendships.'

Research shows that children's friendships are a vital part of growing up and play an essential role in their social and emotional development.[85] Months of lockdown due to COVID-19, when many children have been unable to go to school and only connect with friends online, have had a significant impact. Our children want – and need – positive, stable, loving relationships with the people closest to them. While family is key in this, they also need these relationships with their friends. In fact, children who feel isolated from friends are four times as likely to have low wellbeing as those who do not.[86] Friendships enable children to learn more about themselves, help them develop social skills, and give them a sense of self-worth and confidence.

Friendships are formed from the earliest days. When my children were little, I would do a 'swap' on a Wednesday morning. One Wednesday I'd have a friend's child and the next week she would look after mine. Whilst the fortnightly oasis of peace was wonderful and the playdate was fun, something bigger was at stake. These few hours of play and friendship were building blocks of wellbeing in their lives. In fact, the friendship they formed in those early days was so strong that the boys were best men at each other's weddings.

Even at a young age, children need to have the opportunity to engage in playing with other children. This is important because peer relationships are equal and require negotiation and compromise. Through play with friends, children learn to manage their emotions, and without it they can feel lonely and socially isolated.

As children reach adolescence, their friendships become increasingly important. Speaking of her changing relationship with her 16-year old son, one mum said:

'I know that Barney's friends are important to him, but it's been hard seeing things change. We were so close and he used to tell me

85 'Children and the benefits of friendship', *Life Education*, lifeeducation.org.
86 Haridhan Goswami, 'Social Relationships and Children's Subjective Well Being', *Social Indicators Research*, vol.107, 2012, pp575–588.

everything, but it feels like he has a whole life now with his friends that I know nothing about.'

While our teenagers will always need a loving connection with us, their parents, during the teenage years we move down the pecking order. At this time, they need friends who understand them, accept them and, most importantly, share their perspective on the world. Saavi, aged 15, was not able to see her school friends for many months due to the lockdown. She said, 'I actually cried when I heard that we weren't going to be going back to school this term. The worst part of lockdown for me is not being able to hang out with my friends. I miss them so much.'

Not everyone needs lots of friends. While two of my children have a small number of good loyal friends that they met at primary school, the other two have a much larger group of friends that have changed with the seasons. A study has shown that teenagers who do have a close friendship experience a greater sense of self-worth and that this close relationship offers protection against many of the common mental health issues faced by young adults.[87] Interestingly, the key factor is not the number of friends a person has, but the strength of one relationship. To know and to be known by one other person gives teenagers critical life skills that serve them well for years to come. So as parents, rather than licking our wounds and feeling aggrieved that we've been left out of their lives, understanding the value of adolescent friendships means we can be on the front foot and intentionally foster an environment that helps them make and maintain healthy relationships.

Although strong friendships are vital for children's emotional wellbeing, it doesn't follow that making friends comes naturally to everyone. This is a skill that has to be learned and involves

87 Rachel K. Narr et al., 'Close Friendship Strength and Broader Peer Group Desirability as Differential Predictors of Adult Mental Health', *Child Development*, vol.90, no.1, 2019, pp298–313.

responding to social cues, taking turns in a conversation, responding to body language and tone of voice, and discovering shared interests. I remember a day at the beach when our children were small and were happily paddling in a stream. They were soon joined by two other children and they played with them until lunchtime, building dams and constructing a system of waterworks that would have made the Environment Agency proud. When Charlotte, our daughter, returned to where we were sitting, she told us all about her new best friend, Lucy. Lucy lived in London, she had two brothers, a kitten, a hamster, a goldfish, a pink bedroom and a new butterfly hairclip. Lucy's class teacher next term would be Mrs Webster. The two girls were friends forever. George, our son, returned a few moments later. As no information from him was forthcoming, I enquired about the new friend he'd been digging alongside for the past few hours. He looked puzzled, paused for a moment and said, 'Oh him? He's just a boy.'

Despite the common belief that girls are somehow 'better' at friendships than boys, most boys consider their friends a vital part of their lives. In fact, research shows that boys may actually be better at maintaining friendships: a study of 10- to 15-year-olds found that girls' friendships were actually more fragile.[88] Girls tend to say and do hurtful things to each other more frequently than boys (what psychologists call 'relational aggression'), and they find the end of a friendship more painful. The way boys and girls form and maintain friendships also tends to be different. For boys, friendships are often built around active play like Lego, sports or gaming. 'Doing' things together builds a feeling of connectedness. Whereas for girls, it is more about talking, hugging and sharing every detail of their lives.

Parents of children with additional needs may find their children need extra help with friendships. One mum explained:

88 Joyce F. Benenson and Athena Christakos, 'The Greater Fragility of Females' Versus Males' Closest Same-Sex Friendships', *Child Development*, vol.74, no.4, 2003, pp1123–1129.

'Todd struggles to make friends and I have found it helpful to talk to other parents and give them ideas as to how to include him. For example, whilst he can't join in a football game, he loves throwing the ball back in and he's brilliant at keeping the score.'

Social media sites and gaming can also help children with special needs and development disorders to communicate and make friends. One couple commented on the joy, fun, learning and confidence that their two children seem to have gained from gaming:

'Our oldest has anxiety, and gaming was a way for him to fit in with his peers and does make life easier for him. He's very sociable and it's a helpful way for boys especially to chat, while gaming together.' [89]

Part of our children figuring out how they want to fit in – and how they want to stand out – may mean trying out mixing with different groups of friends. Healthy friendship groups are based on shared interests, sport or music, the youth group, school or family connections. While their members may or may not do everything together, they can come and go and are free to hang out with others in different friendship groups without worrying about being cast out.

Cliques are different. Although they may look much the same as these groups on the surface – they are also clusters of friends formed around common interests – the social dynamics are poles apart. In a clique there is a clear understanding of who belongs and who doesn't and making friends outside the closed circle may result in rejection or ridicule. Children may feel under pressure to behave or act in a particular way or get caught up in bullying or other unkind behaviour. They may even feel victimized, left out or alone.

When things go wrong with friendships, and if our children are worried or pressured by friendship issues or cliques, it's important to resist the urge to try and fix it. Instead, we can concentrate on listening

89 Katharine Hill, *Left to Their Own Devices: Confident Parenting in a World of Screens* (Muddy Pearl, 2019), p16.

to and empathizing with them, trying to see things from their point of view and providing a safe space for them to talk about how they feel. Empathizing with our child can help them feel both heard and understood, and will enable them to move from thinking about the issue in a purely emotional way to a more rational, problem-solving way. It can be useful to ask them to think about how their friends might be feeling, take responsibility for problems they have contributed to, and think about what might make things less stressful next time.

As parents, we can focus on encouraging our children to be friends with people they like and enjoy being with from a wide range of settings, backgrounds, ages and interests. But perhaps, most of all, we can share with them that the secret of making a true friend, someone they can confide in, laugh with and trust, is for *them* to be the kind of friend they'd like to have: loyal, thoughtful, caring, trustworthy and kind.

ACTION POINTS

Best Friends Forever

- *Introduce or encourage your child to meet different children with a common interest.* Children who don't find it easy to make friends can feel more confident with those who enjoy the same activities as them.

- *Help your child say nice things to other children.* This is a really important social skill along with learning to start up a conversation, smiling, saying when they are having fun, and giving compliments.

- *Teach children to give and accept apologies and recognize that everyone makes mistakes.* Encourage them to recognize that real friendship should never end over a small incident. Talk issues out and give each other second chances.

- *Let your child know that friends are welcome in your home.* Make them feel comfortable and accepted, although don't be afraid to ask them to follow any rules you have — for example, asking permission to have a snack, speaking respectfully, or rules about phones at the meal table. Getting to know your child's friends will give you some insight into what they talk about.

- *Discuss peer pressure with your teenagers.* Friends can influence each other in both a positive and negative way. Help your child recognize the friends who will bring them down and don't have their best interests at heart.

- *Give your child plenty of opportunities to mix with other children.* After-school clubs, sharing lifts, school trips and holidays, family get-togethers, scouts, youth groups, sports and especially doing any activities which encourage their talents.

- *Don't pressure a shy child to join in.* If we continually push our more introverted child to make friends or join in with others, we'll only increase their anxiety. While they should not be rude to others, allow them to interact socially at their own pace.

ACTIVITY

Play an acting game with your young child, asking if they want to be themselves or the other child. Then come up with a list of scenarios and work through them. Make it a fun activity. For example:

1. What to do when they want to start a conversation with another child or a group of children.
2. Dealing with a hurtful comment.
3. Going along with another child's suggestion for play.

'Er, Mum, you do realise it's Thursday today?'

CHAPTER 12

IT'S OK TO FAIL

The summer sports camp at the local fitness centre was a godsend to Nick and Michaela. Their demanding jobs took up much of their time and energy, and while they tag teamed childcare as best as they could, two weeks of sports camp offered them much-needed breathing space. What's more, their three boys loved it, so it was a win-win opportunity for the whole family.

James, aged 12, had chosen to do table tennis. Hours of hitting a ball on a table against the garage wall meant he was already a pretty good player, but a week's coaching had raised his game considerably. Towards the end of the second week, a tournament was announced. James knew he had every chance of winning; he was at the top of the age range for his group and, as yet, he was unbeaten. He flew through all the preliminary rounds and the day of the final arrived. The first indication his parents had about how the day's events had gone was the sound of the windows rattling as the front door slammed shut and James hurtled past the open kitchen door. Taking the stairs two at a time he flung himself onto his bed sobbing uncontrollably. Nick and Michaela looked at each other across the kitchen table, neither daring to move. Evidently, the match hadn't gone his way.

Helping our children manage failure is an important task of parenting, but it's not easy. Our every instinct is to swathe them in bubble wrap, cushioning them from disappointment and the hard knocks of life. We long to see them stand on the podium of success, and it can be agony to watch them fail.

Helicopter parents have been the subject of much discussion in recent years.[90] The term describes mums and dads who hover over their children, rotor blades whirring, ready to swoop in at a second's notice to avert catastrophe and guarantee success. Whether leaping in to prevent a toddler's tower of bricks from toppling, micromanaging homework, or driving across town with forgotten permission slips, band instruments or ballet shoes, this style of parenting can take many forms. But while it comes from the very best of intentions, it can backfire. We do our children no favours if we constantly shield them from disappointments or from finding out that life isn't always perfect. Needing to get everything right and not learning to manage failure can lead to a crippling perfectionism and research has shown that this can debilitate children, leaving them either obsessed with achievement or prone to procrastination.[91] In turn, this can then lead to children being vulnerable to anxiety and stress, and unable to deal with failure when it comes their way as it surely will.

As parents, we get to write the script for how our children learn to deal with failure, and our own upbringing will influence our approach. Whilst some of us learnt from our mistakes as part and parcel of everyday life, others will have had few opportunities to fail. Therefore, a good question to ask ourselves is whether we see failure as something that hinders our children's success or as fertile soil for

90 H.H. Schiffrin et al., 'Helping or Hovering? The Effects of Helicopter Parenting on College Students' Well-Being.' *Journal of Child and Family Studies* 23 (2014), pp548–557, doi.org.
91 Jill Adelson, 'A "Perfect" Case Study: Perfectionism in Academically Talented Fourth Graders', *Gifted Child Today*, 2007, no.4, pp14–20.

growth. A 2016 study found that overall, the children of parents who see failure as debilitating rather than enhancing, tend to believe that their intelligence is fixed and that it is not possible to achieve higher levels of attainment through perseverance.[92]

In 1978, basketball legend Michael Jordan tried out for the varsity basketball team at Emsley A. Laney High School. Although he had already shown himself to be an outstanding player, when the team list was posted, his name wasn't on it. The coaches had their strategic reasons for this decision, but 15-year-old Jordan was devastated. In his mind, it was the ultimate failure. He said:

> I went to my room and I closed the door and I cried. For a while I couldn't stop. Even though there was no one else home at the time, I kept the door shut. It was important to me that no one hear me or see me.[93]

Heartbroken, he was about to give up basketball altogether, but it was then that his mother stepped in. Deloris Jordan may not have had a PhD in child psychology, but Deloris was wise. Rather than seeing failure as a source of pain for her son, she regarded it as an opportunity for growth, and she persuaded him to keep going. Jordan decided to pick himself up off the floor and went on to become one of the most famous basketball players of all time. He has since reflected that what made him a winner was his ability to deal with failure. He said:

> I've missed more than 9,000 shots in my career. I've lost almost 300 games. Twenty-six times I've been trusted to take the game-winning shot and missed. I've failed over and over and over again in my life. And that is why I succeed.[94]

---

92 Kyla Haimovitz and Carol S. Dweck, 'Parents' Views of Failure Predict Children's Fixed and Growth Intelligence Mind-Sets', *Psychological Science*, April 2016, doi.org.
93 Bob Greene, 'When Jordan Cried Behind Closed Doors', *Chicago Tribune*, 15 May 1991.
94 Tim Dowling, 'Glass half-full: how I learned to be an optimist in a week', *The Guardian*, 21 November 2019, guardian.com.

Looking back on my own life, I know that my biggest mistakes have undoubtedly taught me more about courage, strength and wisdom than any of my successes. While on the outside, it seems as if nothing beneficial comes from failure, failure actually provides the opportunity for our brains to grow. Both winning and losing trigger the release of different chemicals (dopamine for a win and cortisol if we lose) that encourage new neural connections to be made. A study at Michigan State University found that when children made mistakes in a task, neurons fired in their brains, indicating the formation of new connections. As we have seen in Chapter 8 – 'You Can't Do It … Yet!', children with a growth mindset (a belief that through effort, time and practice they can grow in learning and intelligence), showed a particularly high level of this brain activity when they failed.[95] So when our children have a healthy relationship with failure, their brains can actually grow as a result of it – not in one big 'Aha!' moment, but little by little. If, as parents, we allow our children to experience small failures now, they will learn the skills to deal with, and perhaps even avoid, bigger failures later in life.

Carla told me that this principle of growth through failure was something her daughter, Ella, struggled with. She remembered one particular time when Ella had ripped up attempt after attempt of her maths homework. After yet one more sheet of paper had landed in the bin, Carla felt desperate. She was tired and everything in her wanted to make it easy for her daughter – if she wrote out the answers herself, Ella could copy them in neatly. In the end, she didn't give in to the temptation because she knew there was more at stake than an accurate and nicely presented set of numbers. In a few years' time it wouldn't be Ella's maths homework that would come under scrutiny, it would be the accountancy audit she did at work. And it wouldn't be her teacher she'd have to account to, but her boss.

95 Hans Schroder et al., 'Neural evidence for enhanced attention to mistakes among school-aged children with a growth mindset', *Developmental Cognitive Neuroscience*, vol.24, April 2017, pp42–50.

'One more layer of bubblewrap, just to be sure?'

One of the top 200 TED talks of all time is by entrepreneur Jia Jiang whose story has inspired thousands of young people to deal with failure. Aged 30, Jiang left a dream job in a Fortune 100 company in order to begin a new start-up venture with a guaranteed investment opportunity. But shortly after leaving his job, the investor pulled out. Jiang was devastated but realized that if he was to get back on his feet again he'd need to overcome his fear of failure. After finding a game called the Rejection Challenge, he set himself the task of embarking on 100 days of Rejection Therapy. This involved making outrageous requests to strangers, so inviting rejection and failure. His requests included getting his hair trimmed like a German Shepherd at PetSmart, persuading a bemused Krispy Kreme sales assistant to make him doughnuts in the symbol of the Olympic ring, and asking to participate in a passenger announcement on South West Airlines. He later wrote:

> My goal is to turn rejection into opportunity. I always thought it was something to run away from, but if we can embrace it, we can turn it into a lot more than an obstacle … When you are not afraid of rejection and it feels like you have nothing to lose, amazing things can happen.[96]

Running away from the possibility of failure can put a glass ceiling on our children's ability to grow in strength and resilience. As Sacha and her friends sat in the coffee shop discussing their chances of success in next week's exam, the same phrases were being repeated in cafeterias, changing rooms and corridors across the country: 'I'm going to fail – I just know it', 'I've definitely not done enough work', 'This is my worst subject – I know I'm not going to pass', 'I'm just not clever enough'. These are clear examples of a psychological strategy known as defensive pessimism.

The rationale is simple enough: you lower your expectations, imagining a negative outcome and going through all the ramifications

96 Kate Pisa, 'How to make rejection work for you', *CNN Business*, 20 April 2015, edition.cnn.com.

in your head. In the case of Sacha and her friends, they were thinking the worst about their exams. If they were wrong and passed the exam, they'd be pleasantly surprised. If they failed, not only would they have already prepared themselves, but they'd have the consolation prize of having been right all along.

While this might be an effective short-term strategy for keeping a lid on anxiety, battening down the hatches for protection against a failure that hasn't yet happened is detrimental to building emotional strength. Resilience comes from looking the possibilities of both failure and success in the eye and carrying on regardless.

My husband, Richard, is one of the most adventurous and courageous people I know, but he still remembers the day at school when he was called into the headteacher's office to be told not to apply to a particular university for fear of disappointment if he was turned down. I'm sure that teacher thought he was acting in Richard's best interests, but that kind of approach only builds in children a fear of failure and does nothing to help them learn to use it as a stepping-stone on the path to success.

As parents, we can prepare our children to deal with failure in a way that builds their emotional wellbeing.

1. Encourage them to try new things
Of course we want to encourage our young people to do well in things they are gifted at, but one way to make a stand against our perfectionist culture is to encourage them to take part in activities that they simply enjoy and not where they are necessarily going to excel. I recently spoke to a mum whose daughter had asked to learn ballet. She said:

> *'If I'm honest, she's not really the right build, but I encouraged her to give it a go. I doubt she'll ever pass an exam, and she knows she'll never be picked for the lead role in* Swan Lake, *but I hope she will enjoy it all the same.'*

2. Be a role model

Karl, who is dad to two spirited and competitive boys, told me that he had applied for a new job. The HR manager of the company had phoned him just as he was getting the children's tea to tell him that he hadn't been successful. He had put the phone down and turned to Ben, his 10-year-old, and said, 'Sorry, food won't be for another few minutes – that was a lady telling me that I didn't get the job.' Ben's eyes had grown wide. 'But Daddy, why aren't you crying?' Karl said that it was a great opportunity to explain that while, of course, he was disappointed, someone else must have been a better person for the job and that was really OK. Being vulnerable enough to share our disappointments with our children and modelling how we deal with failure teaches our children a valuable lesson.

3. Stop hovering

Hovering over our children as a helicopter parent can mean that instead of protecting them we are actually robbing them of experiences that can grow their resilience. When my four children were young, my phone was often buzzing with requests from them asking if I would mind 'popping over' (aka drive across town in rush hour traffic) to deliver things like a forgotten book, item of sports equipment, or ingredients for a cookery lesson. I confess I ran the gauntlet more often than was good for building their resilience muscles, but on the occasions I did have the resolve to say no, the children nearly always mined depths of resourcefulness and found creative solutions that otherwise might not have seen the light of day.

Parents of children with additional needs often need the wisdom of Solomon in this area. Ali, mum to Isobel, commented:

> 'Issie sometimes needs me to jump in to protect her, but at other times she needs me to step back and let her learn the hard way. There was a time recently when she was being teased. Another child might have been able to handle the situation, but Issie doesn't have the social skills and needed me to intervene. On another occasion, her PE teacher said

he was going to have to put some consequences in place as she was refusing to join in. I knew that interfering in that one would have made the problem worse. She needed to deal with it herself. It's tough to know which call to make and I often get it wrong.'

4. Show empathy

While a failed driving test or romantic rejection may not seem the end of the world to us, it's good to remember that for a 17-year-old the emotions it engenders can be overwhelming. When life throws our children a curveball, one of the most important things we can do as a parent is simply to listen, acknowledge their feelings, and be there for them.

Failing a maths exam, missing a penalty in the school match or forgetting your lines in the school play may not be the thing that prevents our children from getting a scholarship to Oxford, being selected for the Premier League, or having a career in the West End. But the truth is that they will not get that Oxford degree, land a place in the Premiership, or sustain a future on the West End stage without being able to handle the occasional failure or setback.

I love this quote by author J.K. Rowling:

> You might never fail on the scale I did, but some failure in life is inevitable. It is impossible to live without failing at something, unless you live so cautiously that you might as well not have lived at all – in which case, you fail by default.[97]

Dealing with failure can be painful, but our children will only succeed if they learn the skills to handle what life throws their way. Failure is not what defines us, but how we respond to it will shape us as individuals. Ironically, it is in helping our children learn to fail that we teach them how to succeed.

---

97 Victoria Joy, 'Why failure isn't a dirty word', *The Guardian*, 1 April 2015, guardian.com.

ACTION POINTS

It's OK to Fail

- *Celebrate mistakes.* As a family, create a habit of high-fiving or doing a special dance routine when you make a mistake. This reinforces the idea that failures are not bad, or something to be ashamed of, but opportunities to learn and try harder next time.

- *'What mistakes did you make that taught you something today?'* Asking this question every now and again gives children the opportunity to talk about their failures and the things they are finding difficult.

- *Talk to your children about your own failures.* Much of human learning is based upon modelling, so when we are open about our failures – both past and present – they learn that a failure isn't the end of the world and that being an adult doesn't mean that you always get everything right.

- *Don't try to fix everything.* Give children a chance to find their own solutions to minor problems and frustrations without immediately rushing in to rescue them.

- *Identify your child's strengths and talents.* When a child is aware of the things they can do well, it encourages them to think positively and they gain confidence. Teaching children about their character strengths also increases self-esteem and helps them use these strengths to overcome problems.

- *Every so often have a 'Failure Friday'.* Over a family meal, tell stories of important discoveries or inventions that people made after many failures (for example, Play-

Doh, the ice cream cone, cornflakes, matches, and the Frisbee), or share your own stories of lessons learnt through failure.

- *Provide opportunities to practise failing.* Encourage children to do activities that are fun, not just ones they are good at. As a family, enjoy doing things where there is a high chance of failing – crazy golf or bowling, for example!

ACTIVITY

Hold a prize-giving ceremony on the last day of your family holiday or the school holidays. Prepare little gifts or medals, but instead of awards for the strongest swimmer, the best cook or the fastest cyclist, give prizes that celebrate character. For example, 'The kindest act of the week', 'The person most helpful in doing the household chores', or 'The person who tried hardest to learn a new skill.'

ZIP IT

'You're much better/worse at it than ...'

'It's not monsters you should be afraid of sweetheart.
Global warming and kidnapping are much bigger threats.'

CHAPTER 13

THEY'RE LISTENING

When we've asked our children for the fiftieth time this week to hang up their coats only to find, yet again, a mountain of jackets, cagoules and fleeces strewn across the floor barring access to the kitchen, we might be forgiven for thinking that they don't listen to us. But nothing is further from the truth. They don't miss a thing.

The fact that they are taking in everything we do and say is both good and bad news, of course. They notice how we treat vulnerable or marginalized people, when we are rude or abrupt on the phone, whether we recycle the cardboard from our Amazon order, whether we go back to the shop if we have been undercharged, and how we talk about our difficult mother-in-law (who just happens to also be their granny). And they notice how we react in times of stress and anxiety.

So many things cause us stress as parents. Any fears we already have about the state of the world into which we have brought our children can be easily fuelled by 24/7 news stories of terrorism, climate change, knife crime, grooming and child abduction. Statistics published at the beginning of 2020 revealed that an estimated one in six adults had experienced a 'common mental disorder' in the past week,[98] and since then we have experienced the COVID-19 pandemic. A recent survey of its impact on adults suggests that anxiety, depression, loneliness and self-harm are intensifying.[99] Although scientists have yet to find a single anxiety gene, our temperament undoubtedly makes a big difference to how we handle stress and anxiety. I'm not generally an anxious person, but whenever there are issues in my children's lives that I'm helpless to control, my fears skyrocket.

Professor of Psychology Dr David Anderegg commented, 'Worrying about terrorism is understandable' (and as a parent of children who have been caught up in a coup in Istanbul and terrorist activity in both London and Brussels, I tend to agree), 'but parents worry too much about everyday aspects of parenting.'[100] Of course we want to keep our children safe, but it's easy to sweat the small stuff, become overprotective, worry unnecessarily about things over which we have no control, and allow our children to pick up our angst. Then, it is double trouble because when we parent through the lens of our own anxiety, the chances are that we will pass on this pattern of worry to our children. Ironically, worrying about their children's anxiety is one of the most common reasons parents give for having sleepless nights themselves.[101] We worry – we pass on our worry to our children – we worry that they are worried – they worry even more. The spiral of anxiety and stress becomes uncontrollable.

98 Carl Baker, *Mental Health Statistics for England: Prevalence, Services and Funding*, House of Commons Briefing Paper no. 6988, 23 January 2020, parliament.uk.
99 Libby Brooks, 'Concern for Britons feeling trapped and lonely during lockdown', *The Guardian*, 19 April 2020, guardian.com.
100 Pamela Kruger, 'The Anxious Parent', *Parents*, 5 October 2005, parents.com.
101 Alicia Eaton, *First Aid for Your Child's Mind* (Practical Inspiration Publishing, 2019), p10.

The discovery of special brain cells called mirror neurons[102] in the 1990s has offered scientists new insights into how children learn and reinforces the importance of our being good role models for our children. When we want to do something, neurons in our brain fire up and send messages that allow us to carry out the action. However, the mirror neuron is activated in our brain simply when we *watch* another person's actions and emotions. It mirrors the behaviour of the other person as though they were actually performing the task. Some scientists also believe that mirror neurons play a part in empathy.[103] So how we behave around our children matters – our brains are wired so that we learn by imitation.

Sasha, who has been frightened of driving since she was involved in a shunt on the motorway a few years ago, commented:

'Before I even switch the engine on, I can feel my heart pounding. My hands get sweaty and I get short of breath. As a single parent, I really need to be able to drive, so I try to push through this. Recently, I drove our son Jake to a friend's house. The roads were busy and I became increasingly anxious. The following day we were due to go to the supermarket and Jake refused to get into the car. I realized that he had felt the intensity of my emotions in the car the previous day and was now worried himself. I had passed on to him the message that driving was unsafe.'

Little eyes are watching, and little ears are listening, so while it's no bad thing for our children to see how we manage everyday stresses, we do need to be cautious about sharing the bigger worries of adult life. We can't always prevent worrying things from happening, but as far as possible, we can aim to keep anxious fears from dominating our family life.

102 J.M. Kilner and R.N. Lemon, 'What We Know Currently about Mirror Neurons', *Current Biology*, vol.23, no.23, December 2013, pp1057–1062.
103 Marco Iacoboni, 'Imitation, Empathy, and Mirror Neurons', *Annual Review of Psychology*, vol.60, January 2009, pp653–670.

If we are prone to anxiety, paying attention to how we parent is especially important. Some initial findings from Dr Golda Ginsburg of John Hopkins University show that when a parent is diagnosed with an anxiety disorder, the children are up to seven times more likely to develop an anxiety disorder themselves.[104] This sounds alarming, but the good news is that it's not the whole story.

Having established that anxious parenting puts children at risk of becoming anxious themselves, the researchers decided to create a programme of therapy that would prevent this pattern continuing. Forty families where one or both parents had an anxiety disorder took part in a study in which half were enrolled in the eight-week programme. The therapy was designed to help the parents change their behaviour, in particular focusing on behaviours believed to contribute to anxiety in children, including overprotection, excessive criticism and exposing them to unwarranted expressions of fear and anxiety. Their children were also taught problem-solving and coping skills. The results were powerful. Within a year, 30% of the children in families who had received no intervention developed an anxiety disorder, compared to *none* who had taken part in the family therapy groups.

A useful strategy to help apply brakes to the cycle of anxiety is to ask ourselves the following questions when we are feeling worried:

1. What can I control?
It's natural to want to prevent bad things from happening to our children, but we need to realize that some things are outside our control. Worrying about these is unlikely to change anything; it is more productive to identify the things we *can* have influence or control over and give those our best shot.

---

104 Reid Wilson and Lynn Lyons, *Anxious Kids, Anxious Parents: 7 Ways to Stop the Worry Cycle and Raise Courageous and Independent Children* (Health Communications, 2013), p26.

2. What is real?

The problem with fear and anxiety is that it can skew our thinking and distort facts. It's all too easy to catastrophize – our child failing a Year Six maths test somehow morphs into a prophecy of a failed career in finance, and their not being invited to a party leads to our fearing they will be lonely for the rest of their lives. We can avoid this happening by looking the issue squarely in the eye, examining the hard facts, taming the 'what ifs?', and asking ourselves which concerns are real and which are imagined.

3. What am I really worried about?

Vicky cleared the bank statements from the table and sighed. Since having the children, there was never as much in the account at the end of the month as she thought there should be. They had wanted to go on a family holiday this year, but looking at the bank balance, she couldn't see how it would be possible. The car needed a service and the final payment was due shortly on the furniture they'd bought. She was sure their children's friends at school would all be going away, and she didn't want them to feel they were the odd ones out.

When the phone rang, it was her son, Oliver. 'I've got a detention, Mum. I won't be home until six.' As she got the children's tea, Vicky felt like crying. Oliver was in trouble at school! He'd always been the one she had to worry about least with regard to schoolwork, and now it looked like he was going off the rails … What on earth were they going to do about it? Over the next twenty minutes, her fears about her son mounted, but then she caught sight of the bank statements waiting to be filed and she knew … Oliver was fine. It was only one detention – the first of his whole school career. No, the real worry lay in that paperwork on the shelf, and that was something she'd need to handle with her husband later.

We will all have been there, and I've often allowed my worry about an issue to spill over into something else but taking time to stand back and ask ourselves what the real issue is can help us regain perspective.

4. Who can I ask for help?
If we are parenting as a couple and just one of us struggles with
anxiety, the non-anxious parent can be a valuable source of help and
support. And if we're parenting on our own, it's important to find a
friend who's a calming influence.

Jane is married to Rick, who has suffered from anxiety and
depression for a number of years. Rick describes his anxiety as his
constant companion, always lurking somewhere in the background.
Over the years, Jane has learnt to help Rick manage his anxiety
and recognizes the vital part their relationship plays in helping his
general sense of wellbeing. She reflects:

> *'I haven't always got it right and there have been some painful times,
> but at the end of the day no one knows Rick better than me. In fact, I
> sometimes think I know him better than he knows himself. We've had
> to rely on support from others at times, and counselling has helped
> enormously, but there are things I know I can do that will affirm him
> as a husband and as a dad and help his general sense of wellbeing.
> Focusing on these things has been so important for us in getting
> through together.'*

Rick added that living with anxiety can be a lonely and difficult path,
and while outside help and support is essential at times, what made
the biggest difference is knowing that Jane has his back. 'We're in
this together,' he said, 'and she is there for me come what may.'

Experts find that in some families, an anxious parent will regard
the other as being careless or too relaxed. This can cause the other
parent to go to ground and withdraw from family life in an attempt
not to rock the boat. Mike, whose wife Jen has struggled with anxiety
for most of their married life, commented:

> *'I love the outdoor life and when our kids were young, I'd often take
> them on survival weekends – camping in a remote place, climbing
> trees, swimming in the river, gathering wood, building a fire and
> cooking sausages and marshmallows on it. Jen worried the whole time*

we were away that the children might hurt themselves or be in danger. There were bumps and scrapes, of course, but they loved it. Then on one trip, Billy, our youngest, cut his hand badly whilst playing with my penknife. I had to take him to A&E where they patched him up with several stitches. This injury was all it took to push Jen over the edge – all her worst fears were realized. I obviously felt bad about Billy's hand, but she told me I'd been careless and negligent and blamed me for the injury. I thought it best to keep my head down and we haven't been camping since.'

Rather than stepping back, the best thing a non-anxious parent can do is to step up by positively engaging and modelling to their children a confident, calm presence in the family.[105]

Anxiety has its roots in both genetics and environment and will affect some of us more than others. If it has taken over our lives to the extent that we are living in a constant state of worry and fear, it's important to seek help. It is a common and very treatable problem and certainly not something we have to live and put up with. A first step towards getting help may be to talk about this with our GP.

Anxiety is contagious and spreads invisibly through the home, but when we parent from a place of peace and calm, we will bring a very different atmosphere into the family that affects not just our children's wellbeing but our own.

105 Reid Wilson and Lynn Lyons, *Anxious Kids, Anxious Parents*, p35.

ACTION POINTS

They're Listening

- *Look after yourself.* That well-known instruction given by flight attendants for passengers to put on their own oxygen mask before helping others is also helpful when thinking about our children's wellbeing. If you are struggling physically or emotionally, don't keep this to yourself. Talk with trusted friends and family, and seek professional support if needed. Seeing you address your own struggles in a constructive way is both reassuring for your children and sets a good pattern for them to follow.

- *Tell your children how you are feeling – but within limits.* Children say that they feel less anxious if they are told the truth, and we need to give them information in an age-appropriate way. For example, we might say to our 4-year-old, 'Mummy is feeling sad today because Grandpa isn't very well' and be a little more open about our fears with an older child. Whatever age they are, we must make sure that we don't, in any way, make them feel they are responsible for how we are feeling.

- *Keep adult concerns for sharing with adult friends.* There are things it's not appropriate to burden your children with – for example, problems in your relationship with an ex or current spouse, and work or financial concerns that they do not need to know about.

- *Be careful how you react around your children.* How we respond to a situation, be it an accident, an illness, a disappointment or a worry, will either fuel or dampen their emotions. Make sure not to overreact to something before finding out exactly what is going on and what can be done about it.

- *Take steps not to pass on your fears.* Our fears – for example, socializing in large groups or being scared of dogs – can easily be picked up by our children. As well as taking steps to overcome this for your own sake, avoid sharing these fears with them.

- *Model strategies to cope with stress and anxiety.* Help your children cope with their own triggers and pressures by teaching them strategies such as deep breathing and muscle relaxation, journaling, or going for a walk or other form of exercise.

ACTIVITY

Decorate a shoe box and cut a slit in the top to make a family worry box. Encourage your child to write down or draw the things that concern them. Talk about it together, put it in the worry box. At the end of the month, sit down together and read through these. You and your child may be surprised to see how many of the worries took care of themselves.

'THERE. I'M OUTSIDE. HAPPY NOW?!'

CHAPTER 14

BE BODY CONFIDENT

Gemma and Scarlett had been looking forward to the leavers' prom for months – it was the highlight of the school year (which is why the cancellation of proms in the wake of the pandemic has been such a blow to teenagers). Several afternoons in town had resulted in the purchase of outfits to die for and now the big day had arrived. Parents who have survived the school prom experience will know that for the children concerned, the preparation rituals often afford at least as much (if not more) fun than the event itself, and as soon as lunch was over, the girls were ready to begin.

In fact, the majority of children from 13R were engaged with beauty regimes in full swing (face masks, waxing strips, hair straighteners and eyelash curlers hard at work), and mocktails (and where they could get away with it, cocktails) in hand. Hours later, the results were admired by delighted friends as they posed for selfies with hands on hips and red-lipped pouts. After much debate, the most flattering were selected, filtered, edited and posted on their Instagram stories for adoring followers. And this ritual was not just the preserve of girls. The boys of 13R may not have had quite so many beauty products to choose from, but an equal amount of planning, effort and hair gel had gone into perfecting their appearance for the prom.

Of course, there is nothing new about the fun of dressing up for a party, but for today's teenagers the presence of social media gives it a darker side. A survey into the impact of social media platforms on young people's emotional wellbeing found that image-heavy platforms such as Instagram, Snapchat, Twitter and Facebook all had a negative impact on children's emotional wellbeing, especially that of girls.[106]

Ellie, aged 14, follows various celebs on Instagram. She said, 'I love looking at the posts of them with their clothes and make up – they look so cool. My mum keeps telling me that the pictures aren't real, but I don't care. I just want to be like them.'

In a culture where we are surrounded by digitally-enhanced images of the so-called perfect body (with blemishes erased, necks and legs lengthened, and body shapes altered so that they bear no relation to real life), it's unsurprising that our young people feel under pressure about their own bodies. Many simply don't have the ability to apply the necessary critical filter, taking these images at face value, and this leads to spiralling feelings of dissatisfaction about how they feel about themselves.

A survey of 11- to 16-year-olds found that 79% said that how they look is important to them and over half often worry about this.[107] This matters, as the value that young people place on their appearance is closely linked with their overall feelings of self-worth and wellbeing.[108] And worryingly, dissatisfaction over body shape and size isn't just the preserve of teenagers. Concerns about body

106 Jamie Ducharme, 'Social Media Hurts Girls More Than Boys', *Time,* 13 August 2019, time.com.
107 'Somebody Like Me', *Be Real Campaign*, January 2017, berealcampaign.co.uk.
108 Patricia A. van den Berg et al., 'The link between body dissatisfaction and self-esteem in adolescents: Similarities across gender, age, weight status, race/ethnicity, and socioeconomic status', *Journal of Adolescent Health*, vol.47, no.3, September 2010, pp290–296.

image can start as early as 3 or 4 years of age when children are already becoming aware of societal pressures to look a certain way. A quarter of childcare professionals have experienced children as young as 3 labelling themselves as 'fat' or 'ugly', and it's not unusual for 6-year-olds to talk about dieting. Primary school girls are more likely to compare their appearance with their peers, while boys are more likely to focus on how strong they are, usually in relation to how good they are at sport.[109]

The body image that our children consider 'normal' will, of course, be influenced by our family and culture, and especially by the media. Unrealistic portrayals of thin bodies on products aimed at children send out damaging messages. Disney has been criticized for slimming down popular characters like Minnie Mouse and Daisy Duck, while the body proportions of its princesses have also been called into question.[110] More children report worrying about their appearance than about other areas of life, and statistical tests comparing data from 2009–10 and 2017–18 suggest there was a significant increase in the proportion of boys unhappy with their appearance.[111] Boys are now under increasing pressure to sport the six-pack gym body, and girls to have the Kardashian bum, size zero waist, or whatever Hollywood body shape is currently in vogue. This messaging for our teenagers is especially damaging coming, as it does, at a time when they are making the tricky transition out of childhood and feeling vulnerable and self-conscious.

Sian recalls the fraught experience of taking her daughter Izzy and her friends shopping for jeans. Izzy had hit puberty a little earlier than many of her peers and was slightly chunkier in build than her stick-thin friends. 'Comparing herself to her friends and

109 Rachel Pells, 'Children as young as three worry about being fat or ugly', *The Independent*, 31 August 2016, independent.co.uk.
110 Tara Culp-Ressler, 'Kids Start Struggling With Body Image Issues Earlier Than You May Think', *Think Progress*, 21 January 2015, archive.thinkprogress.org.
111 'The Good Childhood Report 2020'.

then to the media images was so unhelpful,' Sian commented. 'Even if she'd given up cakes for a whole year she was never going to be the same shape as them. She is just a different build.' In the car on the way home, whereas her friends were chattering and clutching their purchases, Izzy sat in stony silence with nothing to show for the trip. 'As soon as we got back,' Sian said, 'she shut herself in her bedroom and nothing I could do would persuade her to see sense.'

Many adolescents struggle with 'body image discrepancy' – the term used to describe the gap between how they see themselves in the mirror compared to what they believe to be the ideal.[112] And digital technology has been quick to come to their aid with apps available to narrow waistlines, pump up biceps, whiten teeth, cover spots and make a host of other 'corrections' that enable them to create the very best version of themselves. The danger of this, of course, is that another gap develops – this time between what they see in the mirror and the image they have generated online. Along with the worry that they won't be able to live up to the self they have created, if there is any doubt in their mind about the merits of their photo, instant feedback in the form of comments and likes won't leave them guessing for long.

Lois, aged 15, said, 'At the weekend, I went to the beach with my friend Liv. I looked lush in my bikini and posted a picture. Em posted one as well. I didn't get half as many likes as she did. I think taking the picture sideways on made me look fat, so I deleted it.'

Fourteen-year-old Alex is small for his age and has been teased at school and bullied online on account of his size. His dad has noticed that he's become obsessed with body building – sneaking into his older brother's bedroom to use his weights when he thinks no one is looking. Yesterday Alex asked his mum if she would buy him some protein shakes.

Bullies aren't very creative when it comes to insults. A UK

112 Shannon Michael et al., 'Parental and peer factors associated with body image discrepancy among fifth-grade boys and girls,' *Journal of Youth and Adolescence*, vol.43, no.1, January 2014, pp15–29.

Government Survey found that children's most common experience of serious bullying in school related to appearance. This included physical characteristics such as being tall, small, having freckles or red hair, and, in secondary school, additional issues to do with appearance such as unfashionable clothes, accessories and hairstyles.[113]

In an age where the world's message to our children is that their worth is linked to their dress size or their BMI, parents have a key part to play in instilling in them a healthy body image and sense of wellbeing.[114] Growing up with three brothers, my daughter quickly learnt that gentle teasing is part and parcel of family life. But during adolescence our teenagers will be more sensitive to comments about the way that they look, and it's worth thinking about how seemingly playful comments can cross the line and have a negative impact and damage confidence. One study of adolescent girls found that over half had experienced weight-based teasing from family members, particularly girls who weighed more.[115] Online surveys by the Mental Health Foundation with YouGov also showed that 29% of young people (21% of boys and 37% of girls) agreed that things their family said have caused them to worry in relation to their body image.[116]

Sometimes the solution is a little closer to home. As in so many areas of parenting, the issue of body image holds a mirror up to our own lives. In family life, it's surprisingly easy to find ourselves making offhand comments about our bodies, or passing comment (positively or negatively) about others' appearance. Remarks about

113 'No Place for Bullying', *Ofsted*, June 2012, assets.publishing.service.gov.uk.
114 Stephanie R. Damiano, 'Development and validation of parenting measures for body image and eating patterns in childhood', *Journal of Eating Disorders*, vol.3, no.5, 2015, biomedcentral.com.
115 Dianne Neumark-Sztainer et al., 'Family weight talk and dieting: How much do they matter for body dissatisfaction and disordered eating behaviors in adolescent girls?', *Journal of Adolescent Health*, vol.47, no.3, September 2010, pp270–276.
116 Mental Health Foundation, *Body Image: How We Think and Feel About Our Bodies* (London, 2020), mentalhealth.org.

ourselves or about family, friends and celebs can easily slip into our conversations at home: 'I feel so fat in these jeans', 'I'm sure she's lost weight – she looks great', 'He needs to fill out a bit', 'She looks much better with her teeth straightened', 'Just look at that tattoo/haircut/ eyebrow – what was he thinking?'

While seemingly harmless or funny, a running commentary on looks can give children the underlying message that our appearance is the most important thing about us. And if we are continually critical of other people's bodies, they learn to apply the same criticism to themselves. As parents, being a role model for our children may mean that we need to work on our own body image so that we feel comfortable with who we are. We also need to be mindful of how we express our feelings about our body to our children.

Of course, parents have a responsibility to guide their children with regard to healthy eating and exercise, but when we focus less on weight and body shape in our conversations and compliments, we can break the habit of reinforcing beauty stereotypes. Psychology professor Renee Engeln suggests committing to having a 'body talk free' household: 'When you shut down all that body talk, you leave room for healthier, more affirming and more interesting conversations. You also send your children the message that what matters is not how people appear but what they do and what they say.'[117]

While both parents have a vital part to play in encouraging children to have a positive body image, research shows that positive support from fathers makes a special difference for both boys and girls, and serves as a buffer against them having poor body image.[118]

Whether our children are tiny or tall, shapely or straight, ripped and rugged, or slender and slight – and whether or not their frame

117 Caroline Bologna, '10 Everyday Ways to Foster A Healthy Body Image in Your Child', *Huffington Post*, 25 March 2019, huffingtonpost.co.uk.
118 S.L. Michael et al., 'Parental and peer factors associated with body image discrepancy among fifth-grade boys and girls', *Journal of Youth and Adolescence*, vol.43, no.1, 2014, pp15–29.

conforms to the current fashion ideal – as parents, we can be a positive influence in giving them confidence about their appearance. Researchers have found that an emotionally warm, positive and supportive home makes the biggest difference in helping our children to develop a healthy body image and as a result, positive self-worth.[119]

I will always remember one occasion when we were on a family holiday in West Wales. Our boys were glued to a cartoon and Richard asked our daughter, aged 7, if she'd like to go out with him for a Coca-Cola and a packet of crisps. She was delighted. But instead of grabbing her shoes and coming straight away, she disappeared for the best part of fifteen minutes, only to reappear wearing her favourite red-checked pinafore dress and new sunglasses, having helped herself to a squirt of my perfume on the way.

'*Wow!*' Richard said. '*You look lovely!*'

'*Thank you, Daddy,*' she replied. '*I dressed up for you.*'

And she had.

This is not about throwing the baby out with the bathwater – particularly if our son or daughter has made a big effort, they still need to hear our compliments. Of course we want our children to be healthy, but the key is not to focus on body shape or weight and not to let that be the only thing they hear us praise them for. We can give them the message that they are so much more than their latest selfie and that we value the many other positive qualities in their life – their smile, their kindness, their initiative, their creativity and all the things that make them unique. These are the qualities that don't require them to continuously chase after an ever-changing cultural standard of beauty, the qualities that lead to confidence, positive self-esteem and emotional wellbeing.

119 Ingrid Holsen, Diane Jone and Marianne Birkeland, 'Body image satisfaction among Norwegian adolescents and young adults: A longitudinal study of the influence of interpersonal relationships and BMI', *Body Image*, vol.9, no.2, March 2012, pp201–208.

ACTION POINTS

Be Body Confident

- *Have a body talk free household.* Commit to not criticizing the appearance of other people, yourself, or your children. If we are critical about our own bodies or those of other people, our children will learn to apply these standards to themselves.

- *Avoid labelling food 'good' or 'bad'.* Assigning moral value to foods can induce feelings of guilt or shame and increase the likelihood of eating disorders.

- *Let them experiment with how they look.* Part of the great journey of self-discovery in teenage years is trying out new styles and becoming members of different tribes. Let them experiment; it's all part of working out who they are.

- *Don't immediately counter your child's negative self-talk about their body.* Listen for why they might feel this way – peer pressure, social media, etc.

- *Ditch unhealthy diets.* Both for our children and for us, it's far better to enjoy eating great healthy food and focus on positive steps like exercising and trying new things, than to starve ourselves or create obsessive rules.

- *Focus on what our bodies can do, rather than how they look.* Model appreciation of what the body can do by valuing and respecting your own body and celebrating achievements in sports, dance, etc., both your children's and other peoples.

ACTIVITY

Spend an hour or so going through magazines or social media images with your teenager and guessing which ones have been photoshopped, which are fat-shaming, and which are pure propaganda messages. It's a great opportunity to talk about body confidence and the narrow way in which 'beauty' is portrayed in the media.

ZIP IT

'You're looking a bit tubby.'

HEALTHY BODY, HEALTHY MIND

EXERCISE

Our minds and bodies are not separate entities; how we treat one impacts the other. Exercise is helpful not only because it improves our physical health, but also because it burns off unwanted stress chemicals and increases our levels of feel-good endorphins. This doesn't have to mean forcing our children to undergo intensive gym workouts! Studies show that children who simply spend more time outdoors and in nature are calmer, happier, have better sleep patterns and perform better at school.

- *Anything is better than nothing.* Just getting outside and moving is always worth it; it doesn't need to be intense and it doesn't need to cost money. Walking, running, skipping, cycling and swimming are all great for improving strength, balance, fitness and concentration.

- *Think outside the box.* If your children don't love school sports such as football, netball or cross-country running suggest they experiment with other activities to get them moving such as martial arts, ice skating, rock climbing, dancing, skateboarding or even synchronised swimming!

- *Use exercise as transportation.* Take a second to think if you really need the car for that journey to their piano lesson. Could you walk together instead? Or cycle?

- *Get involved yourself.* A great incentive for getting children exercising is if we do it with them – and it's a good way of spending time together.

- *Indoor antics.* Turn up the music and make weekly chores into a workout, dance along with Nintendo Wii, or join an online workout.

- *Channel their competitive spirit.* Suggest organising a mini-olympics during the holidays or setting up a garden assault course and provide prizes as incentives.

- *Consider planning a holiday around exercise.* Whether it's hiking, mountain biking or surfing, a holiday involving outdoors activities can be more relaxing and harmonious than a week listlessly lounging around a pool.

- *Encourage team sports.* As well as increasing children's self-confidence and cooperation, they're also a great way for them to develop new friendships outside school. Research has also shown that organised sports can help children develop trusting relationships with safe adults.

- *If you don't know where to start, try your local library.* They are one of the best places to find out what facilities are available in your area.

'Don't you just love a good old-fashioned family meal?'

I'M THERE FOR YOU

One of the most effective ways to build our children's emotional resilience is for them to be sure that while we may not always agree with them, sometimes disappoint them, and sometimes have to discipline them, we will always be there for them.

At our Care for the Family parenting events, people often ask 'Which is the most important: quantity time or quality time?' My answer is that it's both. In my experience as a parent, we often have to put in quite a lot of quantity time in order to get those quality moments. When food needs to be on the table in twenty minutes and the chicken drumsticks are still in the freezer, World War Three is erupting over the PlayStation console, and an urgent email has come in from our boss, quality time with our children is the last thing on our minds. But research shows it is worth fighting for – spending time with our children helps their emotional wellbeing.

Child psychologist Dr Margot Sunderland says:

> Repeated daily good connections between parent and child foster what is known as secure attachment, or resilience … Research shows that it leads to better functioning, a stronger immune

system, better physiology, higher academic marks, a sense of wellbeing and contentment – and it prevents mental and physical ill-health in later life.[120]

We live busy lives and it can be easy to overlook the fact that the simple act of spending regular time with our children contributes to their feeling of self-worth. In our image-conscious world where children measure their value by the number of streaks or likes they have on social media, prioritizing a few minutes with them when there are a million and one other things we could choose to do, gives them the message that they matter. *How* we spend the time isn't important. It can be just hanging out. The key is that *they* and not the activity are the focus of our attention.

One dad I know regularly takes his 7-year-old on a trip to the carwash. 'It has become the thing we do together,' he said. 'I think the fact that it's the carwash is irrelevant; we could go to the tip, to B&Q or to the garden centre. The important thing is that it's just the two of us.'

It can be challenging to intentionally carve out time in our busy schedules, but time with our children doesn't mean we have to find 'extra' time. We can make everyday moments such as car journeys, mealtimes or standing in queues all count. A more herculean task is the need to show up emotionally as well as physically. The smart phone in our pocket has the advantage of allowing us to be in touch 24/7 with our family, friends and office, but the flip side is that we disconnect with the person right in front of us. Ironically, with the pressures of living together, week in, week out, during lockdown, many parents have found it even more difficult to maintain this emotional connection with their children. Pippa, a mum of three, reflected:

'I learnt an important lesson the other day from my 6-year-old. We were doing a jigsaw together, but I wanted to keep an eye on how the bidding was going for something I was selling on eBay, so I kept

120 Tim Cumming, 'Why spending time with the family is more important than ever', *The Telegraph*, 29 June 2018, telegraph.co.uk.

nipping out of the room to double-check my laptop. When I came back after the fourth time, my son said, 'Mummy, you're not really here, are you?' '

My own children are now in their late twenties but, to my shame, they can all remember occasions when I did the same thing on family film nights. I made a value judgment that deleting text messages or editing my profile was a better or more productive use of time than simply sitting with them and watching the film. But the message I was giving my children was that those activities were more significant to me than spending time with them. They were not important enough for my sole attention.

While filming Care for the Family's parenting course *Parentalk*, we interviewed Jon, a dad with two boys aged 8 and 10. He had a demanding job and to keep his inbox under control he took full advantage of his smartphone's access to emails. One of his boys did not see Jon's phone in the same favourable light. As Jon was replying to some emails one Saturday morning, he heard his son ask him a question, but he wasn't really listening and didn't reply. His son persisted. 'Daddy, can we go to the park? … Daddy?' Irritated, Jon looked up and said, 'Can't you see I'm busy?' In sheer frustration, his son replied, 'You were a much nicer Daddy before you got your iPhone.' Ouch!

A few yards away from our house there is a primary school and recently a procession of parents and children caught my eye as they arrived for the first day of term. Forcing smiles and murmuring reassuring words, mums and dads held their phones outstretched as they carefully recorded the moment their child stepped into a new season of life. As I took in the scene, it struck me that these children would have been looking at the back of their parents' phones since the day they were born. And I understand why. Just this morning, as my grandson was engrossed in building a tower of bricks, I found myself spending more time on my phone capturing his skill as a budding architect than I did getting down on the carpet and playing with him. Of course, we want to capture the first smile, the first step, the first day at school, but if we aren't careful, we actually miss it. We treat it as just another photo opportunity rather than a special moment of connection with our child.

Whenever I am asked to speak about the importance of parents spending time with their children, I invariably tell the story of our family tradition of breakfast at Tesco's. (I now have families from all over the UK saying that they are doing a similar thing. One day, I should write to Tesco's and ask for some commission!) With four children and a busy household it was difficult for Richard and I to find opportunities for one-to-one time with our children, so when they were quite small we began the routine of one of us taking one of them to breakfast at Tesco's on a Saturday morning.

As well as giving our children the precious gift of our time, those breakfasts allowed us to check on how they were doing generally. We didn't often talk about anything in particular; the Aston Villa football score or latest Top Shop essential might be the height of the conversation. But every now and then, often when we least expected it, they would open up about the deeper things going on in their lives – maybe the fact that they were struggling to make friends, had been the butt of an unkind joke, or that they were worried about something.

For those parenting alone with more than one child, the opportunity to give one-to-one time can be especially difficult. Kat, a single-parent mother, said that it was easier to do when the children were older. She used to go shopping with her teenage daughter and played pool with her teenage son a few times. Although she was rubbish at it, he really enjoyed it and they had fun together. With younger children, Kat offered this advice:

> If you have family or friends who can look after your other children while you spend time with just one of them, do take advantage of this. If there is no one who can do this for you, consider rotating one-to-one time with each child every Friday night while the others watch a film on TV.[121]

121 Kat Seney-Williams, *Surviving and Thriving on the Single-Parent Journey* (Lion Books, 2019), p81.

A friend whose daughter often seemed overwhelmed with the ordinary pressures of life told me that when it felt like things were spiralling out of control she would call 'Time out' and suggest that Anna went to her room to calm down. With hindsight, my friend said that the much better approach would have been to call 'Time in'. If she'd let Anna stay in the room with her, it would have communicated to her daughter that she was there for her.

While one-to-one time is important, spending time together as a family also pays dividends. And although adverts for theme parks and expensive days out might suggest otherwise, family time doesn't need to be expensive and exciting. We should also recognize that this isn't a sugar-coated ideal. Inevitably, there will be film nights when the film is rubbish, bike rides that are disrupted by punctures, and board games played with missing pieces and rows over the rules. All these are part of the rich tapestry of family life and weave a sense of belonging and togetherness in our children's lives.

When I look back on my children's childhood, the times together that I thought were disastrous are often the ones they remember with fondness. The truth is that children often see things very differently to adults and have different metrics of success. The story is told of a famous man who planned a special day's fishing with his son. That evening, he wrote in his diary that he thought the day was a dead loss. His son had seemed bored and preoccupied, saying very little, and the father decided he probably wouldn't take him fishing again. The boy grew up to be famous in his own right and years later a historian found the son's diary entry for that same day: 'What a perfect day it has been,' he'd written, '... all alone with my father.'

As adults, the lens through which we view the world is different to that of our children. So even if, to us, the time we spend with them feels unproductive, to them it is a message that they are valuable enough to warrant our undistracted attention. And the memory of this means that whenever trouble comes their way, they'll know that we'll be saying 'I'm there for you.'

ACTION POINTS

I'm There for You

- *Quality time and everyday tasks.* When it's possible, invite your child along with you when you are doing routine tasks such as taking the car to the garage, posting a letter or going shopping. Often, the best conversations can happen by chance in situations like these.

- *When possible, be physically present for homework or instrument practice.* For some children, particularly younger ones, the background presence of a parent when they are doing homework or practising music skills is reassuring and helpful.

- *Have a TLC day for your teenager in times of high pressure.* When you know they are stressed out, take some of the pressure off by cooking their favourite food, giving them a break from the day's chores, and arranging for them to do something fun.

- *Share a hobby or other pastime.* Fishing, going to football, watching a film, long walks, jigsaws, photography – the sky's the limit.

- *Eat together.* Try to have a meal together a few times a week as your schedule allows. It's an opportunity to connect with each other, celebrate, commiserate, tell a story and feel part of the family.

ACTIVITY

Have a regular 'date' with your children. Arrange one-to-one time with one child doing something they enjoy – playing pool, going swimming, going shopping, have a Saturday morning breakfast.

'You just push those feelings right down until
you're in your mid-forties, ok?'

CHAPTER 16

IT'S OK TO FEEL SAD

Mollie, who is now in her twenties, has struggled for a number of years with acute anxiety and depression, leading to self-harming and suicidal thoughts. Her mother, Lizzy, reflected on her efforts to support her daughter through those difficult years:

'School presented big issues for Mollie – particularly the sixth form. She would come home either depressed and feeling she couldn't cope, or mad at her teacher or school in general. One day she had a detention for wearing a nose piercing to school (which was against the rules). Furious with what she saw as the unfairness of the situation and how she had been 'picked on', she was overwhelmed by the strength of her feelings. In an attempt to help, I remember interrupting her and trying to present a different perspective with comments along the lines of 'Just calm down and don't be so angry about it', 'You know it's school policy – your teacher isn't picking on you', 'You'd make life so much easier for yourself if you just followed the rules'. Instead of defusing the situation, I lit a touch paper. She stormed out of the kitchen slamming doors behind her and retreated to her bedroom. A couple of years later, and with several family therapy sessions under our belt, I realize that my approach was not what she'd needed. I'd

been so desperate to defuse the situation that I'd jumped in to try to snatch away her feelings before she'd even had time to voice them. I now see that what she really needed was for me just to be there, ask her how she felt, listen to her responses, and reflect these back to her. My desperation for her to be OK, and in particular for her not to be unhappy, had blinkered me to this. I've now been able to change my approach and it has transformed our relationship.'

As human beings, we all face stresses and traumas, some of which are no more than hiccups – short-lived irritants or pressures – and others that are far bigger. How well we deal with these and our ability to bounce back, plays a major part in our mental wellbeing.

When a child has a difficult experience, they will probably default to one of two initial responses, neither of which are helpful. They may internalize or repress their feelings, which can lead to self-blame and depression, or they can externalize or express their feelings in an unhealthy way through aggression, lashing out and blaming others.

As Lizzy discovered, a third and better way to help children handle stress or trauma is to simply allow them to be upset. It is only then that they can begin to problem-solve and take control. When our children are sad or angry, we need to help them 'hold the emotion' by acknowledging their feelings. Once we have done this, we can then help them stand back from the issue and find a solution. This process is important because it is how they build emotional muscles that will stand them in good stead for when the next challenge comes along and the process begins all over again.

When our children were small we went on holiday with friends who had children of roughly the same age. While ours all had their moments, the tantrums of one of our friend's children put her in the running for an Oscar. With arms and legs flailing and screams at decibels that could be heard in the next county, this little one erupted into explosions of temper at any time and any place – the museum, the shopping centre, the beach – saving her best performances for the supermarket queue. However, my Oscar nomination went not to her but to her mum. During these outbursts, my friend remained a model of patience and calm. In her situation, I know that the weight of disapproval from passers-by would have sent me first begging, then bribing my child to be quiet, whereas this amazing mum looked unruffled and composed. Standing by to make sure her daughter didn't come to any harm and let her know that she was there for her, my friend simply let the tantrum run its course.

I believe her ability to take her daughter's tantrum in her stride was particularly heroic not only because, like all parents, she didn't want to see her child struggling, but because of the messages that our culture gives us. First, we have been sold the belief that family life is always a heavenly nirvana of peace and happiness. This means that we see our children's outbursts as an unwelcome interruption and quickly jump in to smooth them over. It's an approach that leads to what has been called 'a fragile rigidity' – the fear that strong emotions could shatter us – and is the very opposite of resilience. However, if we want to build resilience in our children's lives, we must begin by understanding that difficult emotions like sadness or anger aren't a problem to be fixed but part and parcel of being human and an essential part of family life. Tears are not necessarily a bad thing. In fact, they act as a safety valve by releasing excess stress hormones. As Gandalf says in Tolkien's *The Return of the King*, 'I will not say: do not weep; for not all tears are an evil.'[122] Allowing our children to experience a full range of emotions is vital to their wellbeing.

The second myth we buy into is that our success as parents is defined by how happy our children are. If they are happy, we must be good parents; if they are unhappy, we are at fault. It's no surprise then that, to keep our egos intact, we rush to prevent our children experiencing any unhappiness.

When children vent their feelings of frustration and anger, it is often their parents who take the hit, but whether it's a toddler

122 J.R.R. Tolkien, *The Return of the King: The Lord of the Rings Part 3* (Harper-Collins, 2011), p284.

tantrum or a teenage tornado, there are some practical things we can do to help our children deal with their feelings and bounce back.

1. Pause to breathe

Research has shown that parents and children often synchronize their heart rates and breathing,[123] so pressing the pause button, refusing to panic, breathing slowly and staying calm, can not only help us deal with the situation but have a measurable physical effect on our child.

2. Show empathy

Rachel Simmons, the author of two bestselling books about adolescent girls, writes: 'Adolescents … have, as girls like to say, "all of the feels." They have feelings to spare, feelings they could sell on eBay.'[124] And it is the tsunami of these teenage feelings that are often dumped on us as parents. We are caught in the crossfire, left feeling dazed and seeing stars. But as hard as it is to be on the receiving end of all that angst, rather than our ability to swoop in and fix the problem, it's our ability to listen and to empathize – to validate their feelings – that will matter most to our children.

It's no small task to sit on our hands whilst our children struggle, and indeed it's not always possible (or even desirable); in some situations, our children will need our immediate intervention and help. But it's important to remember that struggling is key to learning at every age. As adults, most of us realize that the important life lessons – those that made us wiser and stronger – were those we learnt in the difficult times.

It's not good for our children to be sad all the time, of course, and if we suspect there is a long-term problem, we need to take action. But for many of us, it may come as a relief to discover that it's OK for our children to struggle, and that when they do, simply being there for them is enough.

123 Michelle Woo, 'How to Handle a Public Toddler Tantrum', *Lifehacker*, 28 June 2019, lifehacker.com.
124 Rachel Simmons, *Enough As She Is: How to Help Girls Move Beyond Impossible Standards of Success to Live Healthy, Happy, and Fulfilling Lives* (Harper Collins, 2018), p194.

'Give me a minute. I'm deciding whether to express or repress.'

ACTION POINTS

It's OK to Feel Sad

- *Don't minimize your child's feelings.* Ignoring or making light of how they feel won't make those emotions go away, and they need us to see and acknowledge when they are in pain or struggling. Expressing this verbally – for example, 'I saw you fall off your bike and that must have really hurt' – will help them to feel safe. On the other hand, denying their feelings by saying something like 'Don't be silly; the film isn't scary', can make them feel insecure and bury their feelings deep inside or act them out through other behaviour.

- *Accept that you might need to feel sad too.* It might be easier for us if we jump in to save our child from tears and frustrations, but as long as they are not in danger, let them work through their feelings on their own, even if seeing them struggle makes us feel sad. It's a life skill, and practice makes perfect.

- *Don't give the impression that happiness comes with 'things'.* If our reaction to our child being unhappy is to offer them a new toy or a trip to the cinema, we're teaching them that a lack of happiness can be put right by things that come from outside.

- *Share your own experiences with your children.* Talk to them about times in your own life when you were sad or disappointed. As they grow older, you may be able to share with them disappointments that you are currently facing and what you are doing to help you get through.

- *Protect crying children from others who want to call them a cry-baby.* Children need to know that crying is a good, healthy way for people to express their sad feelings.

ACTIVITY

Ask each member of the family to choose their favourite 'feeling sad' song that they can play during times when they need to let out their feelings. Have it available on your phone to play for younger children, or suggest that older children download it on their own device. Not only will it be cathartic for them, but it'll be a useful alert to the rest of the family that they are feeling emotionally fragile at that time.

It's also a great way to teach boundaries in expressing sadness, by providing a properly defined space for your children to let themselves be sad, express their feelings, then pick themselves up and get on with life.

ZIP IT

'Don't be a drama queen!'

'I'll be sitting Tom's exam. He's rubbish under pressure.'

CHAPTER 17

YOU'LL BOUNCE BACK

Phil answers the door and signs for the delivery. Great, it had arrived. He had decided to order a surprise for the kids as they'd had to cancel the family holiday. He shouts 'Hi kids, come and see what I've got for you!' Harvey, aged 6, and his 9-year-old sister Tamara hurtle down the stairs and wrestle the packages from his arms. Ripping off the cardboard, they discover two kits to build their favourite dinosaurs – a Tyrannosaurus Rex for Tamara and a Diplodocus for Harvey. They run into the living room and tip out the contents of the boxes onto the floor. Tamara lays the pieces out in order, and Harvey tries to copy her. She begins to clip her skeleton together, but Harvey can't figure which pieces go where and gets more and more agitated. Phil realizes he's struggling, so steps in to help.

Phil: *'Harvey, that's a great start.'*

Harvey: *'No, it's not Dad. It's stupid. It looks all wrong. I can't make things like Tamara. I'm no good.'*

Phil: *'That's not true, Harvey. You're a brilliant model maker. Hand it here and I'll make it for you.'*

Harvey: *'OK. Mine never work.'*

Phil is intervening because he can't bear to see his son struggling, but in doing so he is making two mistakes. First, he isn't being truthful. Harvey's attempt at making a dinosaur isn't going to be as good as his sister's – mainly because she is 9 and he is 6 – and Harvey knows that. But second, and more significantly, in taking over and making the dinosaur for his son, Phil is giving him the message, 'When you can't do something, just give up and let someone else do it for you.'

I made both of those mistakes many times. I remember nominating one of my children as Star Baker in a family *Great British Bake Off* competition even though his cupcakes looked like something you might find on the bottom of a shoe, particularly in comparison with his sister's creation, which would have given Mary Berry a run for her money. And I once found myself researching glacial flow at 10pm for geography homework due in the next morning. Each time I acted with the very best of intentions – to help whichever child it was – but in fact I was doing the opposite. I was doing nothing to further their competence or, more importantly, build their resilience.

A scientific definition of resilience is 'the ability of a substance or object to spring back into shape',[125] and in the context of families, for decades it was described as the ability to 'bounce back' and recover from a setback in life. Today, professionals have given resilience a broader meaning; rather than 'bouncing back' it is also about 'bouncing forward'. In other words, it is about not only getting back to normal after facing difficulty, but learning from the process in order to deal with the next challenge that comes along.

Resilience is key to our children's wellbeing. Resilient children tend to be more optimistic and motivated, think more creatively, develop strategies for problem-solving, enjoy good friendships, communicate well and have higher self-esteem.[126] It used to be

125 Resilience, n., *Lexico: Oxford English and Spanish Dictionary, Thesaurus and Spanish to English Translator,* lexico.com.
126 'Literature Review: Resilience in Children and Young People', *The Children's Charity,* June 2007, actionforchildren.org.

thought of as a characteristic that was more or less set in stone; but whilst some children will be more naturally resilient than others, professionals now view it as a skill that can be learnt.[127] So how do we teach this important quality to our children?

A friend recently told me of a wonderful conversation he had with his 7-year-old son. It went something like this:

Son: *'Dad we learnt about resilience in school today.'*
Dad: *'That's great. What did you learn?'*
Son: *'That resilience means bouncing back.'*
Dad: *'And what is bouncing back?'*
Son: *'... I don't know – we haven't learnt that bit yet.'*

While classroom initiatives to teach about resilience are welcome, visual aids using balloons, bouncing balls or putty will only ever convey the theory. The truth is that resilience can really only be learnt in the context of the hard knocks of life. Developmental psychologist Ann Masten describes the development of resilience as 'ordinary magic',[128] meaning that it doesn't happen as a result of a mountain top, earth-shattering event, but in the grit of perseverance during the common struggles of life. As parents, however, allowing our children to do difficult things and then seeing them struggle with or fail at these can be hard.

Five-year-old Tom has been given a new bike for his birthday and can't wait to try it out. In the park with his mother, he zooms off along the path, careless of looking where he is going despite her warning to look out for potholes. Fifteen minutes later they are back at home with Tom sitting on the kitchen table as his mother applies copious amounts of kitchen roll to his grazed knees. An important test will come the following morning. Tom's mum can see that he is in two minds about going on his bike again, and at the thought of him possibly inflicting more damage on his battle-scarred knees

127 'Building children and young people's resilience in schools', *Public Health England*, September 2014, assets.publishing.service.gov.uk.
128 Ann Masten, *Ordinary Magic: Resilience in Development* (Guilford Press, 2014).

she is sorely tempted to simply put a stop – at least for the time being – to any further attempt. But even as they both hesitate, she knows that what Tom does next will be important in building his emotional resilience. He needs to learn from the experience and bounce forward – in other words, to get back on his bike, and, this time, look out for the potholes!

Twelve-year-old Aaden is heartbroken when his guinea pig dies. His mother doesn't want him to have another pet as she can't face going through the trauma again, but his dad persuades her to change her mind. Sitting down with his son, he talks with him about how upset he's been and asks Aaden how he might feel if another pet died. He would still be sad, of course, but he'd know what to expect, and at least that would make the experience easier.

Fifteen-year-old Clara has been having singing lessons and dreams of making it big in the world of musical theatre. Since she was given a major role in the school production of *Grease* she has never missed a rehearsal and spends hours practising her part on her own at home, week after week. Then suddenly, the day before the concert, the school are informed it has to be cancelled. Clara is devastated and cries for two days. She feels so angry and upset that she resolves never to let herself risk going through that let-down again. She thinks to herself that it was stupid of her, anyway, to have believed she could be a successful performer. She stops going to her singing lessons despite her teacher's and parents' best efforts to persuade her otherwise.

The key to resilience is mindset: how we think about whatever setback we are facing. Our children's first reaction on facing a challenge that seems too hard is often to get into a loop of negative thinking, blaming others or themselves. As parents, we can encourage their thought patterns to default to a loop of positive thinking where they will see challenges or problems as opportunities to problem-solve and develop new skills.

So a 'resilience building' version of Harvey's dinosaur challenge might look something like this:

'Yummy! Just the way we like toast!'

- Harvey experiences the stress of being unable to build his diplodocus.
- He gets frustrated and blames himself.
- Instead of intervening, Phil steps back.
- He suggests Harvey thinks of some new ways of tackling the problem.
- Harvey owns the process.
- Together they sort out the pieces and work out how to build the dinosaur.
- Harvey tries again and now has some valuable problem-solving skills under his belt.

As parents, many of us love to control our children's circumstances, and of course we want their lives to be as stress-free as possible. If the experience of living through a world pandemic has taught us anything, it is that we aren't in control, and the reality is that they will experience knocks and setbacks every day. They are unlikely to be able to build every model, pass every test, win every match, succeed in every job interview, and find that the path of true love runs smooth. We can't, and shouldn't, remove all the challenges, but we can help them see negative events as part and parcel of everyday life and pass on skills to help them cope with stress and adversity.

Steven Pete was born with the rare genetic disorder congenital analgesia, which means that he cannot feel any physical pain.[129] He grew up on a farm, and while his parents did their best to protect him, he was continually hurting himself, often seriously. In a BBC interview, he spoke about the bones he had broken as a child and how he was in some form of plaster cast almost continuously until the age of 12. The lesson of his story is sobering: although it hurts, pain serves a purpose. It's easy to be duped into believing that all pain in our children's lives is negative and needs to be avoided. But if

129 'Congenital analgesia: The agony of feeling no pain', *BBC News Magazine*, 17 July 2012, bbc.co.uk.

we give them the message that they are only going to manage when free of pain, we set them up for heartbreak and, ultimately, failure. The truth is that an appropriate level of pain and difficulty serves a positive purpose as the catalyst for building emotional resilience.

Care for the Family runs some incredible activity holidays for single-parent families and one of the highlights is the high ropes course. Ten-year-old Abi talked about the first time she attempted this – it's a great example of the process of growing resilience:

> 'When I put the harness on and looked up at how high it was, I didn't think I could do it. I was scared and started to cry. But John [the instructor] was so kind, and he encouraged me to try. I was really slow, and I felt bad that everyone behind me was waiting, but my mum kept talking to me and cheering me on – and I did it! I felt so happy, and I can't wait to go back next year and try it again.'

Clinical psychologist Meg Jay likes to describe resilience as a heroic struggle: 'It's really a battle, not a bounce – an ongoing process that can last for years … [it's] not a trait. It's not something you're born with. It's not something you just have.'[130] The lessons that our children learn about resilience when they are young, will set them up for a lifetime process of dealing well with whatever challenges are thrown their way.

Harvey, who is now 16, turns over the paper for his DT exam. The task is to design a bird table. He has built a coffee table before but has no idea how to approach this new task. His heart starts to race and he begins to panic. But then he takes a deep breath and a hundred experiences come into play – not just the day his dad brought the Diplodocus home, but all the other times since then when he didn't know how to do something but had tried anyway.

He picks up his pen and begins to write.

130 Meg Jay, '8 tips to help you become more resilient', TED, 5 January 2018, ideas.ted.com.

ACTION POINTS

You'll Bounce Back

- *Set earning goals.* In our on-demand culture, we're encouraged to avoid the discomfort of waiting, but delayed gratification has a positive effect on physical and emotional wellbeing. Instead of just buying that much-desired PlayStation game or new bike, suggest that your child saves up for it with pocket money or extra money from chores. Work out a timescale, write down how much they've saved, and put it up somewhere visible to keep them encouraged.

- *Give children opportunities to take on everyday challenges.* If we never allow our children the chance to do something that is difficult for them – and perhaps to fail at – they won't persevere with other things when they get tough. Struggling to climb to the top of the playground spider web or working out how to use a new computer programme are things we might want to prevent or quickly sort out for them, but if we do this, we deny them the satisfaction of solving something for themselves.

- *Allow natural consequences.* As long as it's safe, letting your child experience the outcome of an action or behaviour is a valuable part of helping them learn. If they forget their sports kit, missing the match will teach them more than you frantically jumping in the car and driving to school with it. It's not always comfortable to go through as a parent, but it's a real resilience-builder for them.

- *See the funny side.* When things go wrong in your own life, set an example by accepting them with good grace and even seeing the funny side.

- *Teach forgiveness.* Researchers have found that forgiveness is important to our happiness, and unforgiveness can even lead to anxiety and depression. Children who learn not to hold grudges take the initiative to resolve breakdowns in relationships and are able to move on from having negative feelings about the past.

ACTIVITY

Help your child to take responsibility for a setback. When something doesn't work out for them, draw up a pie chart with them and ask them to decide:

1. How much was due to me?
2. How much was due to someone else?
3. How much was simply due to circumstances – for example, not having an essential piece of equipment or being in the wrong place at the wrong time.

'Just fill out these risk assessment forms and we'll make a decision about going to the park.'

CHAPTER 18

STEP OUT

As we sat in stationary traffic on the M25, I remembered why we usually spend bank holidays at home. Our hosts texted to tell us not to worry about the delay; they had prepared a cold buffet, so no soufflés were going to spoil because of our late arrival. Within seconds of stepping through the front door after we eventually arrived, our four children descended on the feast.

Our 4-year-old was particularly taken with the cubes of cheese on cocktail sticks that had been jammed into a potato and made to look like a hedgehog. Minutes later, he regurgitated a half-chewed piece of cheese into my palm. Apparently, it tasted 'dis*gu*sting!' Further investigation revealed that he had a discerning palate: the cheese tasted overwhelmingly of antiseptic. Our hosts' home was known for being pristine; the kitchen was sterile and their attempt to eradicate all known germs had now extended from the work surfaces to the food. I remember the mum being horrified once when I applied the five-second rule to a slice of pizza that had fallen on the floor, dusting it down and giving it back to my eldest (who wasn't, I recall, struck with food poisoning as a result). The interesting thing about this family is that despite their stringent hygiene and spotless home, their children always seemed to be ill; there was no build-up of resilience from germs and they would pick up every cold or tummy bug going. It led me to wonder whether a little bit of household dirt is not such a bad thing after all.

It seems I was not far wrong. A concept termed 'antifragility'[131] has been used to describe properties of systems that are *strengthened* through being exposed to stress and challenge. The banking system, our bones and, of course, our immune systems all have this in common – they get stronger when exposed to stress. Parents who treat their children as fragile by not exposing them to germs or vaccines prevent their immune systems from developing healthily to fight infection. But it's not only our children's physical systems that benefit from an antifragile approach. Exposing our children to appropriate challenge and risk is a vital part of their social and emotional development.[132]

But it's hard to do. First, we live in a risk-averse culture. Twenty-four-hour news reports bringing real time disasters directly into our homes paint the world as a dangerous place and make us sensitive to thoughts that such things could happen to us. Never has this been more true than during the pandemic. While health and safety and safeguarding policies serve a vital role in keeping our children from harm, and have been absolutely necessary to combat the spread of the virus, in the longer term this can lead to a cautious, play-it-safe mentality prevents us from allowing them to step out and take any risks at all.

Second, as parents, we are hardwired to protect our children. I was watching my little granddaughter take her first few tentative steps this week, and her parents' every instinct was to leap in to prevent a fall. The same is true throughout our children's lives. It's difficult for us to grasp that a little risk-taking with the potential for a bump or two is in their long-term interests.

131 Nassim Taleb, *Antifragile: How to Live in a World We Don't Understand* (Penguin Books Ltd, 2013).
132 Peter Gray, 'Risky Play: Why Children Love It and Need It', *Psychology Today*, 7 April 2014, psychologytoday.com.

The 'snowplough parent' – another recently-coined term for a particular parenting style – describes parents who protect their offspring and make life as easy as possible for them by removing all obstacles from their path. But on days when we are tempted to put on our snow boots and start clearing snow, it's helpful to remember the old saying 'Prepare the child for the road and not the road for the child.' When we 'prepare the road for the child', sweeping piles of proverbial snow and ice out of their path, we deprive them of the opportunity to dig through the snowdrifts themselves.

Building our children's wellbeing by allowing them to take appropriate risks is one of the key roles of parents because it helps them become more capable and confident. This, in turn, helps them tackle bigger challenges with assurance and positivity.

Psychologists have found that when they are left to their own devices children spontaneously seek to add risk to their play.[133] I remember all too clearly experiences of my own children exhibiting this trait. Amongst activities such as jumping into the sea from higher and higher rocks and burning GCSE books and school ties on a garden bonfire that quickly went out of control, one incident involved 'trying out' a Swiss Army knife. This resulted in an early morning trip to A&E. As the child concerned is now a surgeon, fortunately all his fingers remained intact.

The appeal of risk dramatically increases in the teenage years due to the way in which the brain is developing. As we discussed in Chapter 2, the rational centre of the brain, the prefrontal cortex, is one of the last areas to fully mature, whereas the area of the brain that seeks out pleasure and reward, the *nucleus accumbens*, develops early on. It is this potent combination in the process of brain development which is responsible for a teenager's desire to bungee jump off a bridge or go biking without a helmet.

133 Leif Kennair, Ellen Sandseter and David Ball, 'Risky Play and Growing Up: How to Understand the Overprotection of the Next Generation', in *Pseudoscience: The Conspiracy Against Science*, ed. Allison B. Kaufman and James C. Kaufman (MIT Press, 2018), pp171–194.

A series of studies showed that teenagers take more risks not because they don't understand the dangers (they generally do), but because they weigh risk versus reward differently to adults.[134] Developmental psychologist Laurence Steinberg used a video game to illustrate this.[135] The object of the game was to drive a car across town in as little time as possible. If the traffic lights along the route were turning from green to amber, participants scored more points if they accelerated and managed to drive through before the light turned red. If they were caught by the red light, there was a penalty. So the game rewarded small risk-taking, but penalized bigger risks.

When the teenagers navigated the course by themselves in an empty room, they took the same risks as adults. But when their friends were in the room watching them, they took twice as many risks as they did on their own (unlike adults, where friends being present made no difference to the risks they took). Steinberg concluded that the risk-taking was heightened not because the teenagers underestimated it, but because of the higher reward it gave them.

It is this heightened need for reward that drives some of the most frustrating teenage behaviour. Combine it with the late-developing rational part of the brain and we have a good explanation for some teenagers wanting to skateboard off buildings, climb up hotel balconies, tombstone into the sea, send that revealing selfie, or watch *Love Island* rather than revise for their history exam.

We know our primary responsibility as a parent is to keep our children safe, so what type of risk is it helpful to allow them to experience as part of growing up? We know our child best, and recognizing the challenges that are right for their stage of development and individual temperament is key. While sending an unaccompanied 3-year-old to preschool on the bus would be foolish, allowing a child who is starting

134 Kendall Powell, 'Neurodevelopment: How does the teenage brain work?' *Nature*, 442(7105), September 2006, pp865–867.
135 M. Gardner and L. Steinberg, 'Peer Influence on Risk Taking, Risk Preference, and Risky Decision Making in Adolescence and Adulthood: An Experimental Study', *Developmental Psychology*, vol.41, no.4, 2005, pp625–635.

'Excuse me, could you help me get the correct bus?
I normally do it with my mum.'

secondary school to do so might be just the challenge they need. Encouraging children to take risks is about learning appropriate life lessons in the context of a secure environment.

Risk-taking is a bit like a muscle – it gets stronger the more it's used – and just as we wouldn't attempt to go from couch potato to marathon-runner in one training session, our children can step out gradually. It's good practice to introduce children to new challenges in stages, and I tried to do this when I drew up a plan for how my children would travel to their new secondary school.

- Step 1 – a lift to school
- Step 2 – a dry run with them on the bus with celebration milkshakes at a nearby café on arrival
- Step 3 – walking to the bus stop with them and waiting until the bus arrived
- Step 4 – letting them go solo

In hindsight, travelling into town by themselves on the bus might not seem a particularly big risk, but at the time it certainly felt like a big deal for them (and for us). Since they left school, all our children have spent time travelling, and I've found myself on the other side of the world unable to wave a magic wand and having to watch them navigate the challenges of missed flights, broken-down buses, stolen passports, lost wallets, fallings out with travelling companions, acute D&V and many more incidents besides. As I think back now to the taking-the-bus-to-school plan years ago, I'm thankful that they at least learnt the basics, but also that they are still learning to take risks even now.

Some children will need to be encouraged to step out, and as parents, we can coach them through this. Maya, mum of three, said:

'One of my children has always found it difficult to take risks and do new things. I often say to her, 'If you do this, what's the worst thing that can happen? Can you deal with that?' Thinking about that question helps her see that what she is worried about isn't really so bad after all and with me cheering her on, she will have a go.'

Haniya, mum to two spirited teenage boys with a wonderful sense of adventure, told me she keeps three questions up her sleeve to ask herself:

1. Are they equipped to manage this on their own?
2. If something goes wrong, what are the consequences?
3. What will they learn from this experience?

She said:

'Number one is a deal breaker. If it's a risk I know they can't yet manage to take successfully, I say no. But nine times out of ten, I'll let them have a go. In that situation, I find it useful to ask them, 'How can I help you do this?', so I am not taking over but doing all I can to help. The possibility of some harm is what makes it a risk, and as long as it isn't stupidly dangerous, I feel that, in general, what they will learn in the process far outweighs any of the worries I have.'

One dad said that when he watches his children climbing trees and doing things he knows carry some risk, instead of shouting out 'Be careful' or 'Don't fall', he tries to be positive and say 'Watch where you are putting your feet' or 'Concentrate on what you are doing.' This helps them focus not on the danger but on the challenge.

When we are tempted to jump in the snowplough and clear away the short-term obstacles, it may be helpful to set our sights on the long-term aim of our children's wellbeing and ask ourselves the bigger question: 'What is the risk of *not* letting them tackle this challenge?'

Psychologists Jonathan Haidt and Pamela Paresky write:

The links between childhood overprotection and teenage mental illness are suggestive but not definitive, and there are other likely causal threads. Yet there are good reasons to suspect that by depriving our innately antifragile kids of the wide range of experiences they need to become strong, we are systematically stunting their growth. We should let go – and let them grow.[136]

136 Jonathan Haidt and Pamela Paresky, 'By mollycoddling our children, we're fuelling mental illness in teenagers', *The Guardian*, 10 January 2019, guardian.com.

ACTION POINTS

Step Out

- *Don't clip your child's wings.* Every child's purpose in life is to gain independence. So when your toddler is developmentally capable of putting their toys away or dressing themselves – let them.

- *Create opportunity for adventure.* Encourage your children to take part in trips, explorations, expeditions – anything that they are really interested in – with the caveat that health and safety risks have been assessed and that those in charge are trusted and fully-qualified. Organisations like Outward Bound and the Duke of Edinburgh Award provide great opportunities for outdoor adventure.

- *Give small, safe, regular choices – the more the better.* Giving choices empowers children and helps them with decision-making: 'Do you want porridge or cereal for breakfast?', 'Do you want to wear your trainers or your wellies?', 'Do you want to have screen time this morning or this evening?'

- *Talk risks over with them.* Children are more likely to try out risky activities when they've talked about and planned for it beforehand. So when it comes to using a knife safely, rather than saying a simple 'Be careful', say something like 'That knife is very sharp and it could cut you. Hold it by the handle and cut down towards the chopping board.'

ACTIVITY

This week, look for opportunities where you can let your child do something that you would normally supervise. As long as it is safe and age-appropriate, encourage them to realize they are acting independently.

'Dad! Grandma's fallen asleep reading to me again!'

CHAPTER 19

IT TAKES A VILLAGE

While I don't believe there ever was a golden age of the family, I do believe that bringing up children was easier when extended family members lived near each other. Families often used to live, if not in the same street, within striking distance of each other, but geographic mobility and family breakdown means that this is rarely now the case. Fifty years ago, when a young mum struggled with a baby who wouldn't sleep, a newly-married couple had the row of a century, or a teenager went into meltdown after being dumped by a boyfriend, it was likely that a grandparent, uncle, aunty, brother, sister or cousin were living nearby and available to give reassurance and advice. Today, many couples and parents feel isolated and alone, and we are the poorer for it.

Our children are growing up in an individualistic culture, where the power of personal control and independent choice are the dominant message. This is compounded by the digital age which, while giving opportunities for connectivity and peer support, is ironically also increasing children's feelings of loneliness and isolation. Research shows that our teenagers are spending more time Instagramming,

Snapchatting and WhatsApping their friends and less time hanging out with them in person.[137] The lockdowns that have come about as a result of COVID-19 mean, of course, that they have spent even greater amounts of time physically alone. This comes at a price. Without face-to-face connection, they have less opportunity to develop social skills, negotiate relationships and build emotional resilience. Our teenagers may know the right emoji to use, but many have no idea how to navigate that emotion in real life.

In his seminal book on the mind, *A Journey to the Heart of Being Human*,[138] Dan Siegel writes about the tribes he studied in Namibia who were happy because of their sense of belonging. He discovered that the mind does not exist in a vacuum or in isolation. It exists and develops in relationship with the environment and people around us. Being part of a community can have a positive effect on our children's mental wellbeing – it provides a vital sense of belonging and connectedness, and it offers extra meaning and purpose to everyday life.[139]

The African proverb 'It takes a village to raise a child' describes how, in contrast to our Western individualistic society, African cultures emphasize community. Raising a family is a responsibility shared by the whole village, and adults are expected to look out for each other's children. The South African philosophy *ubuntu* (meaning 'a person is a person through other people') describes this beautifully. We don't exist in isolation; we are relational beings, and community in its various forms has a vital role to play in building our children's emotional health.

If we are struggling to communicate with a tantrum-throwing toddler or to connect with a teenager who needs her phone surgically

137 Jean M. Twenge, *iGen: Why Today's Super-Connected Kids Are Growing Up Less Rebellious, More Tolerant, Less Happy--and Completely Unprepared for Adulthood--and What That Means for the Rest of Us* (Atria Books, 2017), p80.
138 Dan Siegel, *Mind: A Journey to the Heart of Being Human* (W.W. Norton & Co., 2016).
139 'Connecting with Community', *Australian Government: Department of Health*, 11 July 2019, headtohealth.gov.

removed from her hand, the presence of community brings hope. Rather than calling up Elon Musk and arranging to send them on a one-way trip to Mars, we can look to others – grandparents, friends, mentors, youth leaders, sports coaches and teachers – to come alongside and connect with them.

Grandparents

Some grandparents live near their grandchildren and some are miles away; some are full- or part-time child carers for grateful parents juggling the demands of work and family; and others are managing the pain of the breakdown of their child's relationship. But whatever their family situation, grandparents can have a wonderful influence on the lives of their grandchildren.

When our children were growing up my parents lived nearby, and they were brilliant at proactively finding opportunities to invest in their grandchildren's lives. At my father's 100th birthday party, I was moved to hear our children talking about their memories of spending time with him as children. They spoke of trips to a special cake shop after school, boat trips and outings to the zoo, the chance to look at and handle the precious stones in his geology cabinet, and his wonderful stories. But most of all, their thoughts centred on the fact simply that he was there for them, ready and willing to listen, and always interested. When he died a couple of years ago, I doubt he had any idea of the effect his gentle, benign presence had on building their emotional wellbeing, or of the part he played in laying secure foundations in their lives.

Psychologists have described the grandparent-grandchild relationship as 'emotionally uncomplicated'.[140] Maybe this is to do with the fact that grandparents can have all the fun and opportunity for influence without bearing ultimate responsibility for the

140 Beth Gilbert, '7 Health Boosts Grandparents Give Their Grandchildren', *Everyday Health*, 19 December 2011, everydayhealth.com.

children – they don't need to make sure that music practice is done or that the rabbit has been cleaned out. Whether it's an 8-year-old who has missed out on being picked for the team, or a 15-year-old who has been the butt of a joke on social media, grandparents can give children reassurance, encouragement and wise advice. And, on occasions when our child thinks we are the worst parents on planet earth, a grandparent can be a refuge in the storm, reminding them that even if they feel the world is against them, there's someone who loves them anyway.

In his book *The Sixty Minute Grandparent*, Rob Parsons writes:

> The truth is that most of us – even as adults – crave for somebody who looks for the best in us: someone to whom praise comes more quickly than criticism. An elderly grandmother went to watch her grandson at the school sports day. Tom didn't get into the final of the 100 metres or 200 metres, and he was unplaced in the longer races as well. In fact, the only event in which he looked remotely comfortable was the egg-and-spoon race, but even then he came last. As Tom and his grandmother walked away together, the little boy's head was down until she put her arm around him and whispered, 'You were the only one whose egg didn't fall off the spoon.' That young boy never did make it as a sportsman, but against the odds he did achieve great things in other areas of his life. I'm not surprised: it's hard to fail with a grandmother like that.[141]

School

Children's experience of school can play a vital part in building their emotional wellbeing, providing a network of support and the opportunity to form supportive and nurturing relationships.[142] The

---

141 Rob Parsons, *The Sixty Minute Grandparent: Becoming the Best Grandparent You Can Be* (Hodder & Stoughton, 2014), pp107–108.
142 'Building children and young people's resilience in schools', *Public Health England*, September 2014, assets.publishing.service.gov.uk.

'I think he's trying to communicate his emotions!
One word, three syllables?'

closure of schools has been one of the hardest aspects of lockdown, and although for some, online teaching may have been an efficient way to learn and get through the syllabus, the missing piece has been the presence of those key friendships and relationships.

A key psychological idea is that all behaviour communicates a need, meaning that if a child isn't able to use words to explain a need, emotion or impulse they will, instead, act it out in their behaviour. The importance of having good lines of communication between parents and their children's school is well established. If parents share with teachers what is going on at home,[143] the school can then be better equipped to deal with the child's actual needs, not just their behaviour. Even the smallest thing can affect our children's emotional world – the demise of their hamster, Grandpa being in hospital, the birth of a new baby. Many schools now have systems in place to actively promote positive emotional health and wellbeing within the school community.

I've already said that teachers are, without doubt, my heroes, but not every school suits every child. As parents, we know our children best and what environment best meets their needs, and we need to take action if things at their current school aren't working out for them.

Greg's mum had made the difficult decision to send him to boarding school. The first term didn't go well. He was being bullied, was desperately unhappy, and pleaded with her to let him go to a different school. She discussed it with the school and felt that he would be fine after the Head said they'd keep an eye on him and that it would be just a matter of time before he'd find his feet and settle in. During the next holidays Greg was just as unhappy as ever, and when she took him back for the summer term, he refused to get out of the car. She said:

'I thought to myself, 'the school knows best', so with the help of a teacher I managed to peel him off the front seat and persuaded him

143 'Building children and young people's resilience in schools', *Public Health England.*

to go in. Looking back, I realize that I should have listened to Greg and had the confidence to believe that, as his mum, I know him best. When he did eventually change schools, he became a different person. I can't change the past, but I could have avoided much heartache if I'd had the courage of my convictions and stepped in sooner.'

Mentors

As parents, we can look out for trusted adults who can be positive role models and mentors in our children's lives – people such as football coaches, dance teachers, youth leaders and family friends. The word *mentor* comes from the story of Odysseus in Greek mythology. Mentor is an old friend of Odysseus who comes alongside Odysseus' son, the young Telemachus, when he is in a spot of trouble and gives him the benefit of his wisdom and experience. Research bears out the importance of involving wise adults in our children's lives to help bring out the best in them. A Canadian study found that children with positive mentors were more confident, had fewer behavioural problems, showed increased belief in their abilities to succeed in school, and felt less anxiety related to peer pressure.[144]

In fact, one of the most influential factors in how well our children are able to manage setbacks and adversity is whether they have other adults (apart from their parents) to whom they can turn for companionship and support. In this respect, grandparents, godparents, youth leaders and other adult friends are worth their weight in gold. When our teenagers' brains are detaching from us as parents and instinctively they might want to keep things confidential from us, it's even more important they have good people to go to instead.

I will always be grateful to those people who invested in my children's lives when they were growing up, giving advice and

144 'Youth mentoring linked to many positive effects, new study shows', *Science Daily,* 15 January 2013. sciencedaily.com.

support, and leading by example. When one of our boys was younger, a highlight of his week would be meeting up with a youth leader for a Hot Chocolate Mountain – hot chocolate with vast quantities of marshmallows and whipped cream. Alongside a sugar hit, they would chat together about life – football, friends, fears, frustrations. As well as gaining new perspectives, it played an important part in developing his emotional wellbeing.

In an age of grooming and paedophile-fuelled porn, of course we will need to be mindful of the adults we allow to have influence in our children's lives. If we don't know the person well, we can consult with others who do know them. We can also make sure that meetings happen in a public space and that our child's communication with them is kept open. Taking the right precautions is essential, but it would also be a tragedy if fear of an inappropriate relationship robbed our children of a mentoring relationship that will help them grow into emotionally healthy men and women.

Many of us will have had a favourite teacher at school, someone who helped us on the way, an aunt or uncle who took a special interest in us, or a youth leader who inspired and encouraged us. Research identifies the importance of 'turnaround people' like these and says that they are marked by three qualities: they are caring, they have high expectations, and they give opportunities.[145] I recently came across a moving ITV programme about footballer Ian Wright.[146] Unbeknown to Ian, a secret arrangement was made for him to meet the teacher who first spotted his talent for football – Syd Pigden. They hadn't seen each other for over twenty years, and on the way to the meeting Mr Pigden said, 'He probably won't recognize me.' But the second Ian saw him there was instant recognition and Ian was moved to tears. Speaking about his teacher afterwards, Ian said:

145 Bonnie Benard, 'Turnaround people and places: moving from risk to resilience', in *The Strengths Perspective in Social Work Practice*, ed. D. Saleebey (Ally, 2002).
146 'Ian Wright gets a big shock!', *YouTube*, Mitogen, 7 August 2010, youtube.com.

'He was so supportive all the time. He kind of had me as his special guy. Now I realize how important he was in my life – the first main, imposing male figure in my life, trying to guide me on the long road.'

As parents, we can do our best, but we can't meet our children's every need, so allowing others to have an influence in their lives can be a game changer, particularly in the area of building emotional resilience. Somewhere in our child's life will be a Syd Pigden.

ACTION POINTS

It Takes a Village

- *Encourage relationships with other safe adults.* It can feel threatening when a teenager would prefer to talk to someone other than us about how they are feeling, but it's a very natural part of the growing up process. If they have a mentor figure who you know is a good influence on them, encourage your teenager to spend time with them.

- *Create opportunities for trusted relatives or family friends to spend time with your young child.* Going for a meal out or to a local football match, a sleepover or a play date with familiar people will give them confidence and a sense of belonging – as well as a good time. Regularly check with your child that they are OK with this and that they do enjoy this time with those people.

- *Use digital media with extended family members.* If our children's grandparents, aunts, uncles or older siblings live far away, take advantage of digital resources to maintain their connection. Even young children will enjoy a conversation or a bedtime story read to them on Zoom, and older children can link up with their cousins via a favourite social media app.

- *Seek advice from those you trust.* As parents, it can be hard to admit to ourselves that there are times when we're struggling with our children – 'If I was a *proper* mother/father I'd know what to do.' The concept of 'It takes a village' is not just about the positive impact on our children of helpful input from others, but recognises that mum and dad, too, are wise to turn to others for support and encouragement.

- *Get involved in community events and take your child along with you.* School events, community gardens, church or other faith-based organisations, fetes and festivals give you and your child an opportunity to connect with people and work together with them.

ACTIVITY

Collett Smart, psychologist and author of *They'll Be Okay*, suggests setting up a Support Triad of people, activities and places that teenagers can turn to in tough times or when they need help:[147]

1. *Three people* – it might be a grandparent, youth leader or family friend, but at least two of them need to be adults and should be people you trust.
2. *Three safe activities* – things that are healthy and enjoyable and raise their spirits.
3. *Three safe spaces* – for example, the garden, a park, a sports club, a friend's or grandparent's home.

147 Collett Smart, *They'll Be Okay: 15 Conversations to Help Your Child Through Troubled Times* (Piatkus, August 2019).

'I'm beginning to understand how you must feel.'

CHAPTER 20

PARENTING IN A PANDEMIC ... AND BEYOND

During a brief lifting of the pandemic lockdown rules and suitably masked, I was able to take my two grandchildren to the local park. Stopping at our local cafe *en route*, I navigated the one-out-one-in policy, secured a coffee, and we continued on our way. At the park, parents, grandparents and carers carefully observed social distancing, struggling to encourage their toddlers to do the same. As I pushed my grandchildren on the swings, I reflected that these little ones were just a few months old when lockdown began – they have never known anything different. In fact, I've been surprised at how quickly this way of life has become the norm. Even our instinctive reactions have been realigned. Mandi, mum to 7-year-old Ben, commented:

> 'My dad lives nearby, and we're in a support bubble with him. Pre-lockdown, Ben would run to give his grandpa a big hug the moment he set foot in the house. At the beginning of the pandemic, I explained to him why we couldn't now hug. At first, he would run towards his grandpa and then stop himself. Now he doesn't even try.'

COVID-19 has touched almost every area of society – not least our family life. Lockdown has left some people lonely and isolated, while other households have been forced to live in close proximity. Family life has effectively been put under a magnifying glass where both the good and the bad things are intensified. As well as being a catalyst for acts of kindness and generosity, the lockdown has also put relationships under pressure. Small irritations have spiralled into full-blown arguments with all the family feeling the strain.

Research carried out by The Children's Commissioner has shown that for a few children there may have been some positives.[148] For those with a stable family environment, the elimination of 'everyday' worries (anxiety about appearance, bullying, their social lives) meant some children's stress levels decreased during lockdown. One survey reported that the opportunity for extra time together was a bonus for many. In answer to the question 'What has helped you during lockdown?' the answer 'family time' was ahead by a country mile.[149] But for a significant majority, the challenges have felt overwhelming. COVID-19 has exposed the gulf between disadvantaged and non-disadvantaged children, with many vulnerable families facing real hardship. More children are falling into poverty, living on benefits and accessing food banks. Surveys have also found that for children and young people with additional needs and those in Black, Asian and Minority Ethnic communities, the impact has been especially severe.[150]

During lockdown much of life has, of necessity, been conducted around the kitchen table, often via a 23" screen, and the strain can feel unrelenting. Many have suffered the trauma of bereavement, and if parents have lost a source of income, financial pressure has added even more fuel to the fire. For many of those who are

148 The Children's Commissioner, 'Stress Among Children in England During the Coronavirus Lockdown', September 2020, childrenscommissioner.gov.uk.
149 Rachel Brett, 'Youth in Lockdown April–June 2020' in *Youth Voices Project in Essex, Essex Council for Voluntary Youth Services*, ecvys.org.uk.
150 'Coronavirus: impact on children, young people and families – evidence summary', *Scottish Government Publications*, 24 November 2020, gov.scot.

managing the logistics of co-parenting, there have been extra difficulties. Unsurprisingly, this high-octane environment is testing our relationships, and putting our mental wellbeing to the test. Living together 24/7 has aggravated existing tensions, and left stressed parents juggling home-schooling-home-working, or riding the rollercoaster of the teenage years, without their usual support systems and coping mechanisms in place. (After the pandemic is over I'm sure there will be many parents who will think twice about grounding their teenagers for a month!)

For children and young people, the changes brought on by the pandemic have formed a perfect storm. Younger children have missed the structures and routines of the school day – the school run, playdates, sleepovers, birthday parties and sport. Schools are reporting that children that were previously potty trained have regressed back into nappies or forgotten how to use knives and forks.[151] And at the very time our teenagers should be flexing their muscles of independence, they find themselves grounded and in an educational limbo, with life as they know it on hold. Perhaps it should come as no surprise then that one in five children have reported persistent stress during lockdown, which is in itself a predictor for mental health disorders.[152]

Rites of passage represent important milestones in our children's lives and many school leavers feel that COVID-19 has robbed them of experiences that should have been filled with excitement, fun and emotion. Farewells to teachers and classmates at end-of-term events, proms, and transitions to a new school have all been taken away, and there is a sense of loss and grief, often masquerading as sadness, anger or irritability.

Jessie, who was a popular, outgoing 12-year-old, moved up from primary to secondary school during the pandemic without having a

---

151 Rosa Silverman, 'How you can help your children navigate the mental turmoil of lockdown', *The Telegraph*, 18 January 2021, telegraph.co.uk.
152 Children's Commissioner's, 'Stress Among Children'.

taster day at her new school or the chance to say goodbye to teachers and friends. Her mother, Tracy, commented:

> '*I hadn't realised how difficult managing this transition would be for Jess. She has become increasingly on edge and often complains of headaches. Before my very eyes, my outgoing, happy, fun-loving daughter has become anxious, introverted and sad.*'

Mia, who was in her final school year, said:

> '*We had an assembly, where we heard that school was going to close … Then we got to take a few pictures and some people signed T-shirts but not everyone had one because they weren't prepared. It's really sad how school ended so early because I don't think any Year 11s really got a proper last day of school. They didn't get a proper send off like they usually would … It doesn't feel real, it feels like we're in a movie and something has gone wrong.*'

Eleven-year-old Tristan had to isolate after developing coronavirus symptoms. He said:

> '*I had no idea I wouldn't be going back to school. I'm kind of sad because I was looking forward to our school trip. We were going to do lots of outside activities with our friends. I'm going to miss the Year 6 production, which is always really fun. It feels unfair.*'

While no one is immune from the impact of the pandemic, it is our young people's emotional wellbeing that has undoubtedly taken one of the biggest hits. In one study researchers found that whereas in July 2017 one in nine children were experiencing mental health difficulty, this figure had risen to one in six in July 2020[153]. Other research has highlighted COVID-19 related increases in worries about mental health, anxiety, sleep, loneliness, eating disorders and self-harm. And there is a growing body of evidence that suggests the

---

153 'Children Show Increase in Mental Health Difficulties Over Covid-19 Lockdown', University of Oxford Department of Psychiatry, 22 June 2020, psych.ox.ac.uk.

fall-out from the pandemic on our young people's wellbeing could be significant and long-term. Another survey[154] during lockdown of over 4000 children and young people found that:

- 41% said they felt more lonely than before lockdown
- 38% said they felt more worried
- 37% said they felt more sad
- 34% said they felt more stressed
- 33% said they have more trouble sleeping.

When children and young people were asked to select the three feelings most experienced during lockdown:

- 51% said boredom
- 28% said worry
- 26% said feeling trapped.

A growing body of evidence suggests that the fallout from the pandemic on young people's wellbeing could be significant and long term.

Before we add the effects of COVID-19 to the list of things that keep us up at night, it's important to recognize that they are not a prophecy of our children's future lives. We are seeing normal reactions to an abnormal set of life circumstances. Of course, if our children exhibit an ongoing pattern of behaviour and we are concerned, we should seek professional help, but we should also think twice before medicalizing feelings of boredom, frustration, loneliness or confusion. Our 8-year-old not wanting to get out of his pyjamas is not necessarily an indication that he is depressed, and our 15-year-old gaming into the night and raging against the world does not automatically equate to their having an anxiety disorder.

Clinical psychologist Dr Roger Bretherton commented that we think of the generation who grew up in the Second World War not

154 'Generation Lockdown: a third of children and young people experience increased mental health difficulties', Barnardo's, 30 June 2020, barnardos.org.uk.

as a 'damaged' or 'lost' generation but as one of the most resourceful, resilient and stoic, because they learned so much from facing challenges in their youth.[155] In the same way, this generation need not be overwhelmed or damaged by the pressures and challenges of COVID-19. In Chapter 2 we learned that parents are the biggest influence on their children's lives, and if we apply the principles of this book to our time together during lockdown, we have every opportunity to help our children grow stronger, more adaptable and resilient.

However, there are undoubtedly a number of areas where COVID-19 has had specific impact.

School

The closure of schools and transition to home learning has meant many parents have had to become teaching assistants overnight – a role few would have signed up to given half a chance. Teachers are my heroes, and many have gone that extra mile in providing online lessons and additional support. But this has still left a lot of parents having to play childcare tag team with a partner, juggling work emails and video conferencing alongside wrestling with dodgy wifi, refereeing the sharing of devices, and supervising science lessons, spelling tests and Shakespeare. When single parents have had to do this, and more, without any support it has been a truly herculean task.

Adjusting to changes in their education has been hard for our children as well. In fact, the greatest reported increase in stress during lockdown came from worries about school. As one 14-year-old said: 'Online learning is all the boring stuff of school without any of the fun bits.' Lack of structure, boredom, and waning motivation combined with worries about falling behind and simply missing friends have created a potent cocktail of stress.

155 The Mind and Soul Foundation, 'Courage, Wisdom and Growth in Pandemic Times – with Roger Bretherton', 29 August 2020, youtube.com.

Chris, who is dad to 11-year-old Caleb, described hearing a crash from his son's room one evening. Tentatively poking his head round the door, he found Caleb with his head in his hands sobbing uncontrollably. His iPad lay on the floor on the other side of the room, the screen cracked and beyond repair. He struggled with maths, and today the slides in his online lesson were going too quickly for him to take notes and something inside him had snapped.

Girls are especially prone to worry about missing school, whereas the focus of boys' angst is often more around a lack of physical exercise and sport. Josh, who is 14, explained that the most stressful thing about lockdown was not being able to play football. He said, 'I've missed my sport. When I play football I just think about the game and don't have to think about other stuff going on in my life. I can't do that now, stuff feels trapped in my head.'

For some children, the cancellation of their exams has been a great relief, sparing them from a great deal of stress and anxiety in the weeks leading up to them. Sixteen-year-old Becky commented that lockdown had taken away many of the stressful triggers – such as pressures from sixth-form – in her life, and that as well as reducing her anxiety it allowed her to study with less worry: 'The rapidly changing situation confronted my fear of not being in control. I'm now able to adapt to new situations in a much calmer way than before COVID-19'. However, many other children feel robbed by what they see as the summary cancellation of the culmination of two years' work. They are left with a feeling of frustration that they will never know how they would have done. Others feel pressurized that without exams, their final grades are decided by teacher assessment, so every bit of work they now do may count. Reflecting on not being able to take her final year exams, Kimberley commented: 'I worked really hard and the opportunity to prove myself in an exam has been taken from me. I no longer feel in control of my future and I'm worried about how I am going to get a job.'

While issues around schooling are top of the list of things causing stress, Natasha Devon, the former UK Government's children's mental health tsar, brings some words of hope:

> This is a really good opportunity to find your driving force. A lot of people go through their life just chasing things and they never understand what puts fire in their belly. So, I ask teenagers: if there was no such thing as grades ... what would you choose to do with your life? This period of uncertainty represents a really good opportunity for them to work that out about themselves.[156]

Friendships

In a recent survey, 87% of young people agreed that they had felt lonely or isolated during the lockdown period.[157] While most had been able to stay in touch with friends, social contact had been much more difficult to maintain, and 50% reported feeling stressed about not being able to see family and friends.[158]

A study of young people in Bristol found that 63% struggled to cope with the reduction in social contact, agreeing that no amount of phone calls or video chats can replace truly connecting and being with a friend. While 2-year-olds may not have had the opportunity of learning to share the toddler group trike, and primary children have missed games of tag in the playground or giggling in the dark on sleepovers, it is our teenagers that have, perhaps, found isolation particularly hard. The teenage years are an especially important time for relationships to develop, including friendships and new romantic liaisons, and the restrictions have had an impact on this. Teenagers tend to thrive in larger groups, and the restrictions have left many feeling disconnected from their tribe.

156 Etan Smallman, 'Coronavirus lockdown: With exams and festivals cancelled, now is time for teenagers to find "fire in your belly"', *iNews*, 22 April 2020, inews.co.uk.
157 'Covid-19 Autumn 2020 Survey', *Young Minds*, October 2020, youngminds.org.uk.
158 Children's Commissioner's, 'Stress Among Children'.

Research has revealed how lockdown has had a 'funnelling effect' on friendships – circles of friends narrowing due to the sheer effort required to keep in touch.[159] This has caused some young people to find themselves left out in the cold without a 'bestie'.

Rob, the father of 7-year-old Pippa, commented: 'When Pippa realised that she wasn't going to go back to school at the beginning of term she was inconsolable. She really misses face to face contact with her friends.'

Maddie, aged 15, agreed: 'I really miss seeing my friends. You are just stuck with your thoughts. Usually, if you're feeling low you can go out with friends and forget your problems, but when you don't have these distractions, small problems get bigger.'

Online connection

Social distancing doesn't have to mean social isolation and the ability to connect with friends online has been a lifesaver for many. Already digital natives, this generation have been able to use technology to the full, with texting, gaming and video conferencing platforms enabling burgeoning social lives to tick over. As well as chatting with friends, an important anchor in the sand for many children has been keeping in touch with extended family, including grandparents who have become tech wizards overnight.

But as much as the digital age has been a lifeline, it has also come at a cost. News bulletins with sobering statistics, interviews with frontline health workers, and distressing scenes of trauma and grief in the wake of the pandemic are continually broadcast straight into kitchens and living rooms. We want to be kept up to date, but the scale and frequency of information can feel overwhelming. And if that's true for us as adults, it can be even more so for our children. It's easy to put the news on 'just in the background' while we're cooking

159 The exact source (French survey, *La Vie en Confinement*) was not available online, but this article refers to it: https://presse.inserm.fr/en/covid-19-and-con-finement-a-large-scale-french-survey-of-social-challenges-and-health/39099/.

tea, perhaps forgetting that little eyes are watching and little ears are taking it all in. Teenagers will most likely be getting information about the pandemic from time spent online, social media and chatting with friends, and may be finding it hard to make sense of all the messages that they are exposed to. Some will be well informed, others misinformed; some may take it in their stride; others will feel anxious and overwhelmed.

The amount of time children spend on screens has risen exponentially during the pandemic. They tap earnestly through online lessons during the day, and then collapse in front of a film or play on their Xbox at night. This should be no surprise, of course. As one young person commented: 'I have got no social life and I am dependent on technology for entertainment. I am overwhelmed with online stuff to do but want to be outside.'[160]

Body language forms an important part of our communication, and incidences of misunderstanding and resulting conflict while chatting on their app of choice are rife because the subtle nuances and facial expressions that would normally be picked up are easily lost.

Increased screen time may also affect any feelings of inadequacy in teenagers. Although immersing themselves into social media platforms and scrolling through lockdown highlights and celebrity posts may provide an anaesthetic relief to those who are frustrated by being holed up, it can also deal devasting blows to their emerging self-esteem.

The teenage years are the time when young people seek independence and work out their identity away from their parents, but lockdown has made the arena in which they can do this very small. During the pandemic, the reality for them has been life lived 24/7 in the home, a scenario which can feel very grey compared to the colour, vibrancy and energy of the online world. The result is that many choose to make the online world their reality – it feels

160 'Youth in lockdown: In their own words', *Barnardo's*, 16 July 2020, barnardos.org.uk.

'Was COVID-18 this boring?'

more exciting and more connected than the isolation of their actual life at present – and it is in *this* arena that they are working out who they are.

Emotions - ours and theirs

The universal rise in stress levels for parents and children alike during the pandemic has lit the touch paper for more negative patterns of thinking and feeling. While some families seemed to come through the first lockdown relatively unscathed, the attrition of subsequent lockdowns without a clear end in sight has taken its toll on us all.

The lack of routine and constant change and disruption to life has knocked our children's emotional equilibrium. Their reactions will depend on their personality and temperament, but often there has been new and difficult behaviour. Testing or anxious children leave us in no doubt that something is up, with challenging behaviour ranging from yelling to withdrawal. But even the most laid-back or compliant youngster has felt that the rug has been pulled out from under their feet. Some 'speak it out' and others 'act it out', but all have questions that need to be unpacked. Suzi, a mum of three, commented:

> *'It didn't happen straight away, but I have noticed my silly, smiley 6-year-old becoming flatter than usual. He is sleeping more, and I am struggling to get him to join in with things that he used to enjoy such as playing with his hamster and kicking a football around. Getting him to do his schoolwork is virtually impossible. His sister, who used to be a good sleeper, is having nightmares and has become really clingy. To be honest, none of us are doing very well.'*

And in a poignant remark to her mum, 14-year-old Chloe summed things up in these few words: 'I don't think I've ever felt so consistently sad for so long.'

As parents, we are hardwired to protect our children, and both the 'helicopter' and 'snowplough' parents excel at this, swooping in to avert catastrophe and clear the path ahead (see Chapters 12 and 18). But if COVID-19 has taught us anything, it is that there is much in life that we can't control. This realisation has brought with it a heightened sense of anxiety for many parents.

For those who were already anxious, the pandemic may have felt like an emotional nightmare come true. Sam has suffered from anxiety for a number of years, and he describes it as something that is always with him, often leaving him feeling out of control and overwhelmed. He commented:

'My mind can quickly spiral into a series of what ifs. I find myself catastrophizing about the current situation and how it is affecting our children, and before I know it, I feel completely overwhelmed. I'm overreacting all the time to everyday inconveniences and irritations.'

Perhaps one of the greatest challenges in managing the rollercoaster of our own emotions as parents is that there is nowhere to hide. Tamsin, a single parent with two boys aged 6 and 8 commented:

'I realise that the boys have been seeing a different side of me. Usually, when I'm at work they are either at school or with our childminder, so it's been a gear change for them to see me in work mode. The last few months have pushed me to the limit. I've locked myself in the loo and had a good cry more times than I'd like to admit.'

Our children are like little barometers and we cannot underestimate the impact of them being exposed to our emotional reactions. Many of us as parents will be feeling overwhelmed, exhausted, frustrated or worried, but Dr Kate Middleton, a mum herself, gives this advice: 'The single most valuable thing a parent can do for their children is to look after their own emotional wellbeing. It may feel counter-intuitive, but time looking after our own needs at this time is time well spent.'

As parents, we are walking a tightrope when it comes to dealing with our children's emotions. We want them to think positively, but at the same time we need to give them space to express negative feelings. It can come as a relief to know that we don't need to have all the answers. Simply talking to them, listening to their concerns and acknowledging how they are feeling, is the most important way in which we can help our children process what is going on for them and make way for more positive feelings to flourish.

An opportunity to build resilience

As all-encompassing as the pandemic has been, we must remember that it is one chapter of our children's lives and not the whole story. With the right support, they have every chance of coming through the other side happy, healthy and even having learnt something from it.

As we have already seen, different parts of a child's brain develop at different times, and if they can learn to harness the positive power of their minds in tough times it will not only help them navigate the challenges of this season, but more than that, it will increase their ability to use those same areas of the brain in the future, building resilience and growing their capacity to carry that most precious quality – hope.

Lockdown has been an eye-opening experience for 17-year-old Anoushka Aggarwala. As an athlete, she was looking forward to participating in a district-level meet in May and was devastated when it was cancelled. 'In retrospect, I was chasing trivial things; I now realise it was a myopic view,' she said. 'If the Olympics could get cancelled, my race was nothing.'[161]

English teacher Dawn Wilson-North was interviewed on Radio 4's *PM* programme and commenting on her pupils' experience of online learning gave a welcome message of optimism.

When you look at … young people going out into the big, wide world, particularly year 11s, they're going to have gained so many

161 Diya Mathew, 'Covid's children: How lockdown has affected adolescents', *The Week*, 20 July 2020, theweek.in.

skills from what they're doing. They're learning self-reliance: they have to be there, work the technology, use the technology that adults are using. They help each other in the chat; they copy links if people can't quite get on. They're learning resilience. These are all employability skills that they're going to be well up to speed on in a way that perhaps other students wouldn't be.[162]

She cautions parents against gazing at their children with tears in their eyes and talking about how bad things are.

I don't know that endlessly telling [children] how awful things are for them is helping. It's not something anyone would say to a child in ordinary circumstances – 'Your life is a total catastrophe, I'm afraid' – so why do it now? Any parent should be wary of encouraging a child to think of themselves as an eternal victim, a thing with no agency: these are not good foundations for emotional wellbeing. I think pupils of all ages are being extraordinary, and that their actions are saving us all, and that they should be praised to the rafters for it.

Mrs Wilson-North, I agree.

The pandemic is not only an opportunity to help build resilience in our children, but it also gives us the chance to re-evaluate and strengthen all our family relationships. This has been an unbelievably difficult time for us all, but as is so often the case, even in the toughest of times there have been glimpses of 'treasures in the darkness'. Although not the case for everyone, some have been fortunate to have discovered the freedom of stepping off the treadmill of busyness and having time for those they love. Regular family mealtimes together, jumping off the bandwagon of after-school activities, Zoom calls, keeping in touch with grandparents

162 India Knight, 'Stop Telling Children that Lockdown is Harmful', *The Times*, 21 January 2021, thetimes.co.uk.

'Why is no one wearing masks, Granny?'

and friends, evenings in, creative ideas for thankfulness, random acts of kindness, and simply some time just 'to be' have all been hallmarks of this season.

The pandemic has been a difficult time for everyone and for many it has not only been difficult, but painful and traumatic. Whilst this dreadful time in history will surely pass, the truth is that our world has changed forever. Early reports show that it has begun to have a harmful impact on mental health and will do so in the years to come. So how can we best help our children at this time? This chapter is different to others in the book because it doesn't contain a specific parenting principle that will help build resilience – but that's because there is no one magic cure that deals with the impact of COVID-19. We have to apply the principles discussed throughout the rest of this book to raising our children during these exceptional times. For our children, it won't be the only difficult circumstance that life throws at them; they have a lifetime of challenges ahead – broken hearts, testing jobs, ill health, dreams that have been trampled on, friends that let them down. And, however challenging we have found our role as parents in the crucible of the pandemic, as we do our best to coach our children through this unique season, we can be encouraged to know that we will also be equipping them for the journey ahead.

ACTION POINTS

Parenting in a Pandemic

- *Keep regular routines.* Structure and consistency can give our children a sense of normality in uncertain times. Stick with old routines and set up new ones where needed. Routines such as regular times for meals, exercise, play/relaxation and bedtime help children feel safe and secure.

- *Listen and empathise.* Keep communication open and offer reassurance. Teenagers will typically open up on their terms, so seize moments of communication when you can, ask open questions, listen to what their concerns really are, and show empathy. Remember that sometimes the issues bothering them won't be what we expect. It's OK not to know everything, but take their age and temperament into account and try to answer their questions about the pandemic simply and honestly. Rather than focusing on things outside our control, focus on what we do know. Listening and offering reassurance will be especially important at this time when they have additional fears, frustrations and worries (see Chapter 7).

- *Help manage your children's stress reactions.* If possible, try to eke out some one-on-one time and do things that help them relax – play a game, make biscuits, bake a cake, go for a walk or bike ride, watch Netflix. If they are feeling anxious, encourage them to take deep breaths and count to ten.

- *Limit exposure to 24-7 news and adult conversations about the pandemic.* Check in with teenagers and find out what they know and point them to reliable sources to help them gain perspective. Once they have the facts, encourage them to switch to something else – and do the same yourself!

- *Look after your own needs.* Take time to wind down and relax in whatever way works best for you, whether it's soaking in a deep bath or going for a run. If work is stressful, where possible talk to your employer, or try to find ways to pace yourself.

- *Stay in touch with grandparents and wider family.* Ask grandparents to read younger children a bedtime story via an iPad, or schedule a Zoom or a video chat with your teenagers' cousins.

- *Help younger children stay connected with their friends.* For example, arrange a virtual playdate or lunchtime get-together where they can talk to each other while playing or eating. Or help them set up a group chat using an app so that they can share jokes or funny videos.

- *Create a 'quiet' space in the house.* Helpful especially for families where bedrooms are shared, this is a place where anyone can go to be left alone for ten minutes' peace and quiet; for example, a bean bag in the corner of a room, or an armchair turned towards the window to look outside.

- *Find things to be grateful for.* Every evening, ask everyone to think of one positive thing they are thankful for, for example, a fun game of snakes and ladders, a new TikTok dance, finishing a maths project, fixing a dripping tap, or playing in the snow.

- *Do something to help others.* Focusing on others' needs can lift our mood. Write notes or a bake a cake for neighbours or friends. Older children might be able to help pack bags for the local food bank or volunteer in some other way, depending on social distancing rules.

- *Encourage children to take some downtime every day.* Schedule in play or activity times for younger children, and encourage older children to do something to relax.

- *Make a memory bag as a reminder of pre-pandemic days.* Collect together some items that bring back good memories, things you can smell, touch, taste or hear. For example, a shell from a beach holiday, a scarf that smells of Granny's perfume, a photo of a best friend, a Christmas decoration. Encourage your child to take them out when feeling stressed.

- *Get creative with lessons.* Ask your children to help with everyday tasks and combine it with learning. Measuring out cookery ingredients, planting seeds, helping with a DIY job, sorting the recycling – the possibilities are endless.

- *And finally – go easy on yourself.* Take it a day at a time, acknowledge it's tough, lay down the guilt, as far as possible stay calm, and remember that during a pandemic, it's OK:

  * to not aim for 'Outstanding' in home-schooling Ofsted
  * to relax the rules a little on screen time
  * to not have a colour-coded activity chart
  * for your children not to know how 'just to be'
  * for teenagers to be missing their friends
  * for siblings to argue
  * for you to need some time out
  * for you just to be there ... everything else is a bonus.

ACTIVITY

Get the whole family together for a fun time with drinks and favourite snacks and draw up a COVID-19 Family Agreement. The aim of this is to set out guidelines and expectations during the pandemic, especially around how digital technology is used at home.

Encourage everyone to participate, from toddlers to teenagers (even the most grumpy teenager is likely to join in if they know they have a voice and will be listened to). Some of your previous boundaries may no longer work or be appropriate during this time, so tear up the old rule book and write a new one.

Children will have been online during the day for schoolwork, but they also need time to socialize with friends. Rather than focusing on limiting screen time, look at issues such as where and when devices can be used (in the bedroom/at meal times/at night) and what exactly can be done online.

With everyone at home 24/7, talk about where and how you can create some private space for each member of the family, especially teens.

Other things you might want to include in your COVID-19 Family Agreement could include expectations around home-schooling, meals, bedtimes, or how much nagging is in order! Make sure that everything is in line with your family values, and make any necessary age-appropriate adjustments for children of different ages.

Once you have drawn up the agreement, the deal is that everyone signs up to it. It doesn't have to be written down and pinned to the kitchen wall, if that doesn't work for you – simply talking about it is what counts. And when life returns to normal, tear it up and create a new one for a post-pandemic world.

'I'm just reading some reviews to see if I'm enjoying this film.'

CHAPTER 21

A MIND OF THEIR OWN

Sixteen-year-old Angus had just started Sixth Form College. It was the first day of term, and as he sat down for breakfast his parents smiled to themselves; he had clearly made a heroic effort with his appearance. Sporting ripped jeans and a designer hoodie, his hair was gelled to within an inch of its life. It was definitely a 'new look' – light years away from the navy-blue school blazer and tie that had previously been his everyday attire. Subtle variations of this look continued for a few weeks – he grew his hair, tied it in a ponytail, and then grew a beard – then one day he came downstairs clean-shaven and wearing a sharp suit and tie, looking every bit as if he was going to a wedding. His father asked him if he was giving a presentation that day and quickly wished he hadn't. After a few days of the city look, Angus changed his appearance again, then several times more – track suit bottoms and trainers one day, glitter another, Goth the next. Laughing about it, his mum said, 'I think he's loving the freedom of being able to reinvent himself every day. It's like he's trying out different disguises.'

While that is undoubtedly true, something much deeper is going on. Angus is asking the question that lies on the lips of every adolescent – one that is at the heart of what it means to be human: 'Who am I?' A definition of identity that I've found helpful is 'the story we tell ourselves about ourselves' – 'our inner "core"'.[163] And the things that are written on the pages of this story are what give our lives purpose, meaning and emotional stability. Knowing who we are, that we belong, and that we are significant is key to our emotional wellbeing.

The teenage years are a time when young people attempt to establish their identity away from us, their parents. They don't yet know who they are (they aren't meant to), and the process of working this out can be stressful for us as well as them, perhaps because all this inventing and reinventing doesn't take place on a level playing field. Influences on their emerging identity come from many different areas – culture and media, faith and religion, their environment, family, school and peers. Our teenagers ask questions, receive feedback, explore possibilities, choose who to hang out with and in what environment, and adjust their behaviour accordingly. As they work through some of the big questions of life – 'Who am I?', 'Do I matter?', 'What is my purpose in the world?'– our role as parents is to listen to their thoughts, answer their questions, and provide a stable base and reference point for them to return to throughout the process.

While the question 'Who am I?' has never been an easy one to answer, for today's teenagers, discovering their identity in a world of rapid technological change and a fast-shifting culture is no mean task. And for young people working all this through in the context of a pandemic, the task is even harder. The digital age allows young people to invent and reinvent themselves in a carefully curated stream of videos and photographs, all of which is done against the backdrop of social approval and the need to measure their worth by the number of their followers or likes.

163 Glynn Harrison, *A Better Story: God, Sex and Human Flourishing* (Inter-Varsity Press, 2017), p144.

Alec, who is 17, sums up the challenge:

'I think ... social media makes finding one's identity much more difficult. We can force [our] opinions to change based on others. We can love something because someone else loves it or hate something because someone else hates it. Social media has made it much easier to judge someone and can make it harder to keep your identity.' [164]

Fifteen-year-old Kirsten has a 'Finsta' (a fake Instagram account) that she tells me her parents don't know about but which she shares with her friends. Like her, many young people have second accounts on different social media platforms where they can experiment with different personas. But Kirsten is finding that keeping her various identity plates spinning is a full-time job.

Blair, who is also 15, reflected on the different identities he carries every day. To his friends, he is fun-loving and lively – a very different person to the private, introverted Blair he presents to his parents. Then there is uber-popular Blair on social media, Blair with the lads, Blair with the girls, Blair with his teachers, and Blair in the youth band. And somewhere amongst that mix is the real Blair who occasionally makes an appearance when no one else is around – the Blair he needs to get to know.

In their search for identity, young people are given a blank page with no outline plot, no storyboard, no word count, no author guidelines. Society tells them they have complete freedom to write their own story – to choose their identity and determine the meaning of their lives. Elsa's song 'Let It Go' from the film *Frozen*, 'No right, no wrong, no rules for me, I'm free!', is an anthem for our times.

To discover who they are, our children are told that they simply need to look within. But herein lies the problem: with no Google Maps for the route and no guard rails to keep them on track, the options are limitless. They are left dangling in the wind, and the very quest for identity chips away at their emotional wellbeing. Those

164 Vivien Reed, 'Is Your Teen Struggling with Who They Are? How to Help Your Teen with Their Identity In a Digital World', *Let's Talk Teens*, 2018, lets-talk-teens.org.

struggling with their identity can feel insecure and confused, unsure of their place in the world, isolated, and lacking in self-esteem and a sense of belonging.

Life doesn't come off the shelf ready to assemble; we need to base it on something. And the irony is that giving our young people total freedom to choose their identity can backfire, leaving them even more unsure and vulnerable to being defined by others.

American psychologist Jennifer Crocker argues that in order to build a healthy identity and self-esteem we need to raise our gaze, widen the lens, and adopt what she calls a 'part-of-something-bigger-than-me' mindset.[165] In these formative years, perhaps this is why so many of our young people seize on group identities; they want to belong to a gang or a tribe, to identify with a cause. Many have an inspiring sense of social justice and need little encouragement to engage with issues of climate change, racial equality, gender, or poverty. They find purpose and significance in looking beyond themselves, and as parents we can encourage them to do that. Contrary to our culture's prevailing narrative of individualism, research shows that the larger the entity that we can be part of, the more meaning we will find in life.[166]

Research by Dr Martin Seligman, Professor of Psychology at the University of Pennsylvania, found that a key factor in building optimism and resilience in young people's lives was religious hope. I agree with him. He writes: '... one truth about meaning is this: the larger the entity to which you can attach yourself, the more meaning you will feel your life has.'[167] I have written this book for people of any or no faith, but for my own part, I have been glad of times when I could come alongside my children and pray about something that

---

165 Glynn Harrison, *The Big Ego Trip: Finding True Significance in a Culture of Self-Esteem* (Inter-Varsity Press, 2013), p129.
166 Martin Seligman, *Learned Optimism: How to Change Your Mind and Your Life* (Vintage Books USA, 2006).
167 Martin Seligman, *The Optimistic Child: A Revolutionary Approach to Raising Resilient Children* (Nicholas Brealey Publishing, 2018), p42.

'It's called FASHION, Dad. I wouldn't expect you to understand.'

was worrying them. Those times were precious, the possibility of faith giving them not only someone to whom they can bring their deepest thoughts and requests, but a fundamental belief that there is meaning and purpose in life, and that no matter what anyone else thinks of them, there is a God who knows them and loves them.

Whatever our reference point in life, whatever our values and beliefs, as their parents we have a vital role to play in helping our children discover their unique identity. We can be a sounding board for their questions and provide a safe space for them to discover answers, but the greatest gift we can give them is the reassurance that they don't need to 'construct' an identity, because they are accepted for who they are. However loud the voice of culture, however busy the identity traffic going through their minds, our unconditional love for them will be the cornerstone on which they can build their lives.

But unconditional love and acceptance is not easy. Shaved heads or dreads, pot or porn, failed maths tests or positive pregnancy tests – the chances are that somewhere along the way our children may disappoint us. But whilst we may not like or condone their behaviour at times, if we want to build their emotional wellbeing, loving our children unconditionally in any and every situation matters.

This matters particularly in relation to their sexual identity. Sadly, the rate of poor mental health among the LGBTQ community is far greater than the rate in society as a whole,[168] and whatever beliefs we have as their parents, our children's emotional wellbeing hinges on our acceptance of them. This is no small thing. Discussion and questions can follow, but our acceptance and love for them must come first. The alternative is for them to feel our rejection.

Discovering our identity is a process, but many teenagers are keen to nail their colours to the mast and tie themselves down to a particular identity too soon. As parents, we can encourage them to

168 Nathan Hudson-Sharp and Hilary Metcalf, 'Inequality among lesbian, gay, bisexual and transgender groups in the UK: a review of evidence', *National Institute of Economic and Social Research*, July 2006.

take time to learn who they are and to enjoy the fact that everything is up for grabs. Learning who we are takes years, so there is no need for them to feel forced to define themselves before they are ready.

Research has found that supportive and warm parenting helps increase young people's clarity about themselves.[169] This means that one of the best gifts we can give them in establishing their wellbeing is to let them know that whatever they think, whatever they believe, whatever they do, whatever they look like, or however many times they fail, there is someone who loves and accepts them as they are.

We have seen that it is in the context of family that our children grow, not just physically but mentally and emotionally. And as their parents, we really are the biggest influence in their lives, no matter how loud the voice of the culture ringing in their ears and the sighs or rolling of their eyes that may indicate the contrary.

As I said, I don't believe there was ever a golden age of the family, but I do believe that it's harder to be a child today, and it is certainly harder to be a parent. Parenting is not for the fainthearted! Many factors are outside our control and it is good to remind ourselves that we can't do it all. Will we make mistakes? Undoubtedly. Will we have regrets? Of course. Probably no other calling in life requires so much soul-searching and provokes more guilt-inducing anxiety, but there is no other role that brings such joy, happiness and fulfilment. Whatever our situation, we can have confidence that no one knows our child like us or loves them like us, and we can give this awesome task our very best shot.

Emotional wellbeing may be something of a recent concept – a term that our grandparents would probably never have come across – but its significance in our lives is something that we dare not underestimate. Along with experiencing the joys, excitements, hopes and successes of life, our children will also need to face up to

169 Andrik Becht et al., 'Clear Self, Better Relationships: Adolescents' Self-Concept Clarity and Relationship Quality With Parents and Peers Across 5 Years', *Child Development*, vol.88, no.6, 2017, pp1823–1833.

its inevitable frustrations, setbacks, traumas and disappointments. In passing on to them the messages that we have discussed in this book, we can help them develop an emotional resiliency that will stand them in good stead.

We can help them develop *a mind of their own.*

'Everyone says I can be anybody I want to be.
But I think I just want to be me.'

APPENDIX
FURTHER HELP AND SUPPORT

The following organizations have published helpful advice, guidance and resources on the issues described in this book. Specific web addresses obviously change from time to time, so you may need to find the article you are looking for by searching from an organization's home page or a general web browser.

General

Action for Children

parents.actionforchildren.org.uk/emotional-wellbeing
Expert advice for parents on all aspects of parenting, including a section giving advice and activities to support children with their mental and emotional wellbeing, including a one-to-one chatline at selected times.

Barnardo's - Emotional Wellbeing Support Hub

barnardos.org.uk/support-hub/emotional-wellbeing
A range of resources, tools, and videos focusing on parents' and children's emotional wellbeing.

Care for the Family

careforthefamily.org.uk
A national charity that aims to promote strong family life and help those who face family difficulties. It provides parenting, relationship and bereavement support through events, resources, courses, training and volunteer networks.

Childline

childline.org.uk
Helpline: 0800 1111
A free 24-hour counselling service for children and young people in the UK up to the age of 19. Childline helps with any issue that causes distress or concern, whether big or small.

Children's Society

childrenssociety.org.uk/what-we-do/our-work/well-being
Specific support for children who are anxious, stressed or depressed, and for those who can't access mental health services and are at high risk of developing a mental health condition if they don't get the support they need.

Dove Self-Esteem Project

dove.com/uk/dove-self-esteem-project/help-for-parents
Resources for parents and mentors designed to encourage young people to develop and maintain a healthy body image during the transition to adulthood.

Family Lives

familylives.org.uk
Helpline: 0808 800 2222
Help and advice to families going through a difficult time including all stages of a child's development, school issues, support around family breakdown, bullying, teenage risky behaviour, and mental health concerns.

Headstrong

beheadstrong.org.uk
An online space for young people looking at how to get the best out of your mind from a Christian faith perspective. Videos, articles and fun stuff covering all topics around emotional and mental wellbeing from illness to how to lift mood.

Mind and Soul Foundation

mindandsoulfoundation.org
Resources, articles and teaching combining expertise from psychology, medicine and theology to encourage the church to engage with all issues around mental and emotional wellbeing.

MindEd for Families

mindedforfamilies.org.uk/young-people
Advice and information that can help parents understand mental health problems and what best they can do to support their family.

NSPCC

nspcc.org.uk
Helpline: 0800 800 5000
A national charity to prevent abuse, help rebuild children's lives, protect those at risk, and support families. The website includes help and advice for parents and families dealing with mental health problems in everyday life.

Ollee

app.ollee.org.uk
A web app created by Parent Zone designed to be a digital friend for children aged 8 to 11 and to make a difference to their emotional wellbeing.

Place2Be

place2be.org.uk
General enquiries: 020 7923 5500
Place2Be is a children's mental health charity working with schools to improve the emotional wellbeing of pupils, families, teachers and school staff.

Royal College of Psychiatrists

rcpsych.ac.uk/mental-health/parents-and-young-people
Information for young people, parents and carers about young people's mental health and the impact of different situations on their wellbeing.

Young Minds

youngminds.org.uk
Helpline for parents: 0800 802 5544
YoungMinds Crisis Messenger – Text YM 85258. Free 24/7 support for young people across the UK who are experiencing a mental health crisis. Help and support for children, parents and professionals concerned about the mental health of children and young people.

Bereavement

Child Bereavement UK

childbereavementuk.org
Helpline: 0800 02 888 40
Support and information for all those affected when a child is bereaved, and for parents when a child has died.

Cruse Bereavement UK

cruse.org.uk/get-help/for-parents
Helpline: 0800 808 1677
Information on what you can do to help a child or young person who is grieving.

Hope Again

hopeagain.org.uk
Helpline: 0800 808 1677
The youth website of Cruse Bereavement Care. A safe place where older children and teenagers can learn how to cope with grief and feel less alone.

Bullying

Bullying UK

bullying.co.uk
Helpline: 0808 800 222
Information and advice on all aspects of bullying, including a free
helpline and live chat.

Kidscape

kidscape.org.uk
Parent advice line: 020 7823 5430
Advice and support for parents, carers and children about bullying
that is taking place inside or outside of school and the community,
or over social platforms and the phone.

Eating Disorders

Anorexia and Bulimia Care

anorexiabulimiacare.org.uk
Helpline: 03000 111213
Personal care and support for anyone affected by anorexia, bulimia,
binge eating and all types of eating distress, including help for family
and friends.

Tastelife

tastelifeuk.org
Tools, resources and courses aimed at prevention and recovery for
those who struggle with eating disorders and for their supporters.

Social media and online safety

CEOP (Child Exploitation & Online Protection Centre)

ceop.police.uk
Internet safety advice for parents and carers with a 'virtual police station' to report abuse on the internet.

Childnet International

childnet.com
Information for children about the latest websites and services they like to use, mobiles, gaming, downloading, social networking and more. A section for parents includes lots of information about what children and young people are doing online together with useful ways to keep your child safe.

Common Sense Media

commonsensemedia.org
Information, advice, and innovative tools to help harness the power of media and technology as a positive force in all children's lives.

Internet Matters

internetmatters.org
Information and advice to help parents keep their children safe online including issues such as cyberbullying, online grooming, inappropriate content, pornography, self-harm.

Parent Zone

parentzone.org.uk
General enquiries: 020 7686 7225
PARENTZONE to 85258: Crisis Messenger text service providing free, 24/7 crisis support.
Information and support for parents to help them raise resilient children in the digital world.

Safer Internet Centre

saferinternet.org.uk
Advice and support on online safety issues, including an anonymous hotline to report and remove child sexual abuse imagery and videos wherever they are found in the world.

Vodafone Digital Parenting

vodafone.com/our-purpose/operating-responsibly/child-online-safety
Advice, support, and practical 'how to' guides for keeping your children safe online.